Strong
Boys,
Fragile Men

Strong Boys, Fragile Men

A Brokenhearted Boys Struggle to find Manhood

George Hines Jr

Copyright

Dedicated to the girl with the big hair
in the red shirt.

FOREWARD

Tenacious, honest (sometimes to a fault) and determined are a few words that stand out when I think about George's early days of college. Watching him grow during his primitive years of manhood was a rollercoaster ride to say the least, and as his athletic and sometimes life advisor, I had a front row seat to it all.   If I'm honest his confidence in himself was often overshadowed by his equally stronger beliefs in his antiquated roles of men and women at the time.

Over the years however, I've witnessed the evolution of his manhood through his beliefs of what he once thought to be true about men and women to know what he knows to be reality. Experience has definitely been his best teacher. He has always had the ability to connect with many and that coupled with his brutal honesty has helped countless others over the years, including myself.

Too often people walk through life with masks on hiding behind the expectations of others and the falsehood of what they are supposed to be. George has never walked through life that way. In fact, his transparency is what makes him, and his work stands out from the rest.
This book is not a blueprint into manhood but rather the pathway into one man's passage into deeper terrains. If you are looking for a read that will take you on a real-life journey from sexual gratification to salvation this is the one. At the core of it readers will find a story about love. For the Bible says love conquers all. That coupled with *truth* and you have a heartfelt narrative of a young man who is still developing into a cultivated being.

Strong Boys, Fragile Men is an honest memoir that should be read and appreciated for many years to come.

~ LaWanda M. Simpkins, PhD
Undergraduate Mentor via Athletics
NC A&T State University 2007-2010

Table of Contents:

INTRODUCTION

A few years ago, while lying in the bed with Vee, she asked me, "G, why would anybody want to read your book?"

Dang...

Great question!

No joke, I honestly had not ever stopped to consider the fact that people sincerely may not desire to read my work for a number of reasons. Thinking to myself, "seriously? Why would they care? They don't know me. Furthermore, everyone has a story! What makes mine so spectacular?"

This question perturbed me to such a degree that I stopped writing. It seemed hopeless and I felt like I was just wasting my time. That is when I made the decision to just keep writing as a personal hobby and save myself the embarrassment. Then one day as I sat thinking, it occurred to me; "No one purchases anything for others. We buy for ourselves! Sure. If I were selling this book to people with the notion that they should read it because I wanted them to, I would be undoubtedly unsuccessful!" But, if there was something valuable in it for them, they would not only purchase for themselves, they would buy for family and friends!

The thing is: **WE ALL WANT LOVE!** There isn't a person in the universe that I am more hopeful for regarding love than myself! Therefore, I am going to invest in any material that I can to gain a greater understanding of the ever-elusive fantasy that we all know as "REAL LOVE". Strong Boys, Fragile Men will not be a quick fix to your love troubles. It is a very detailed account of the forces that drive our love pursuits. It is a depiction of all the paradigms that shape our thoughts, our hearts and our expectations regarding lasting relational happiness.

Within my story, you will find the universal solution to all your love woes. I'm not guaranteeing that you'll find the love of your life after reading my book. To all the ladies, Strong Boys, Fragile Men is not a cure for penny personality, bad taste, hyper-independence, nagging, or ugliness. Although I will state that being ugly can be remedied with skillful and assertive fellatio, hair extensions or beautiful natural hair, make-up and a great workout regimen. *(All these solutions are temporary though, they still don't render the security that knowing and trusting God does. Yet, so many women result to these tactics instead of trusting in the Almighty)* Fellas, I also must warn you that Strong Boys, Fragile Men will not cure your lack of ambition. It will however provide you with the essential tools necessary to become a man that a woman would love to submit to.

There is no sense in having tools that you won't use! Strong Boys, Fragile Men is exactly what is needed to see with a clear lens into the struggles of young men in a Post-Modern, Egalitarian world. My only hope is that you share this book with a friend, your brother, classmate, colleague, co-worker, boyfriend. Be sure to get it in hands of a young man somewhere. We desperately need to know that we are not the only ones trying to realize manhood in these perilous days.

The absolute truth about Strong Boys, Fragile Men is that I never intended to be an author. I had just arrived at the point in life where I was either going to kill someone or kill myself. I was miserable! To add insult to injury, I had no clue in the world of how I would be able to stay faithful to my wife if I did find her. Clinging to a life fueled by the memory of who I was and the hopeful re-emergence of proudness from my pops; I began to dig for answers.

Eventually, I stumbled upon a conversation... At the age of 18, I went off to college. That's when the war for living the truth began...my mama would call and say

"Hey son, I want you to take 7 days and sanctify yourself. NO SEX, NO NOTHING FOR 7 DAYS!"

Here is the entire tale of how a 7-day pursuit *forced* me to confront all my past, the struggles of my present and run headlong into the assignment which held the promise of my future.

WHO IS George Hines Jr.????

If for some reason you stopped to grab this book, or it was recommended to you; I'm sure you're wondering, WHO IS THIS GUY? AND WHY SHOULD I CARE??? Well, by the end of this book, you'll know exactly who I am. Not only that; you're going to be compelled to pass this along to a friend. Depending on how much hatred you harbor in your heart, you will also want your ex to have a copy! WHAT I AM GOING TO GIVE TO YOU IS THE TRUTH THAT YOUNG MEN JUST AREN'T WILLING TO SHARE. IT'S EMBARRASSING YET EYE-OPENING.

I'm only able to share this because I understand one verse from the Book of Life:

> John 8:32 (ERV): *"You will know the truth, and the truth will make you free."*

Nothing in this world liberates us like the truth.

G.K Chesterton says it this way,

> *"Truth is the most valuable thing in the world. So valuable in fact, that it constantly has to be protected by a bodyguard of lies"*

My personal favorite:

"Truth is incontrovertible. Malice may attack it, ignorance may deride it, but in the end, there it is." ~ Winston Churchill

I am here for one reason, and one reason only! To give you the truth. In doing so, I am excited to also fully gain my freedom from a tumultuous past that has tormented me for far too long.

Ready? Let's Get it!

CHILDHOOD

I was born in Rutherford hospital on December 28, 1987. In a small town called Rutherfordton, which I have told numerous people was named after 19th president Rutherford B Hayes. That's a lie. And now that I think about it, I'm not sure why I would say it. Maybe I'm just amazed at how people light up because they're able to put that American History knowledge to use after all those years. Who am I not to allow people to utilize their education? Far be it from me to begrudge them!

Yep! I was born and raised in Rutherfordton. As a matter of fact, I'm still here today. In the same bedroom I grew up all those years ago. I'll be 30 in December. I would say that my parents and I are roommates, but I can't afford to pay them any rent. But we'll get to all of that later if you'd stop interrupting me! Oh, and just so you don't get lost in the sauce, I have a terrible habit of taking detours...but stick with me, I promise we're going to get there. Like I was saying, I am here in Rutherfordton, North Carolina. New Hope is the set I'm repping (yay yay).

My whole family pretty much lives right here on this same street. We are all super tight. I don't even knock on doors when I go in their houses. Every house on this hill is pretty much home for me. From a very young age, I was a rather precocious kid. I blame it on my mama. She always had another book for me to read. Every day after school ma would make me and my friends sit down on the front porch and read. Me being the genius young kid that I was, told her one day, "aye look ma! I know you trying to help us out, but you're going to run all my friends off with all the reading."

Of course, she didn't listen. Eventually, my friends began to wait me out. They would stay at the bottom of the hill until I finished reading. Back then, I despised her for it. Today, I couldn't be more thankful. She used to always say "God gave parents before he gave children." Every once in a while, she would make a good point. It's funny, I don't ever recall my mama making my sister read books. Maybe I was too young to remember. I will never forget the WORD reports she'd assign me after I called my sister a name.

What is a word report? A word report was punishment for calling my sister any name that was intended to hurt her feelings. I had to define the word, use it in sentences with proper context and lastly, I was instructed to tell why or why not this is a good name to call someone. It was abuse! Again, I hated ma back then! But look at me now ma, I'm writing a book. God has an incredible way of weaving our lives together. From the age of 7 ma spoke heavily about responsibility. She hammered and hammered and hammered and hammered and hammered and hammered. Can you name a second grader who wants to be or even cares about being responsible???

I got in trouble so much in school that the school stopped suspending me. They would call Ms. Filmore, my eventual third-grade teacher, and the only black educator I ever had from K-12 other than my PE teacher in high school. At the time, I had no idea that Ms. Filmore was so close to my mama, but I did find it very uncanny how she seemed to say the exact same things ma would say about being responsible. Blah Blah Blah! All my family swears I never got any whippings (which we pronounce as "whooping"), but I feel like I was getting thumped errday! (not a typo)

Overall, Ma was pretty cool and her methods pretty effective. My pops though?! HAHAHAHA! Pops is the man. Superman! (The grammar check thinks that my subject and verb are having a disagreement. SMH... "Pops" is singular.) He introduced me to the truth. The most memorable day of my childhood came on a random evening. I was in the back seat explaining something to my pops. Not sure what I said wrong, but I'll never forget the interjection as long as I'm alive;

"AYE BOY! IF YOU DON'T KNOW WHAT YOU'RE TALKING ABOUT, SHUT THE HELL UP!"

I was 6!!

From that day forward, even until now, anything that I speak on, I know an extensive amount about. Ironically, many people think I'm a "know it all". Blame my Pops.

The very first address I knew growing up was 1600 Pennsylvania Avenue. Everyday pops reminded me "that's where we're heading". He's always instilled major confidence in me. Nothing bothered my pops. He was hardcore. And I wanted to be just like him when I grew up. My daddy was the exact opposite of my mama. Mama was a creative prayer warrior and my pops was more like Def Comedy Jam; truthfully aggressive and unrefined.

He taught with emphasis that the male appendage was a DICK! It wasn't a "pee-pee" or a "private part" or a "ding-a-ling". Dick, it is...thanks pops! We were spoiled children growing up. If we wanted it, we had it. Heck, we thought we were rich. I didn't realize we weren't until I got to college and witnessed all these young girls driving better cars than my folks did. All things considered, we had a tremendous childhood. Sure, my sister caught me hunching a few times. Yes, one day I literally got my draws, some say "drawers" in a wad and had to try to explain to my grandma why I was outdoors with my pants down. WE WERE "HELL" as the old folks would say. Now that you have a brief intro to my childhood, we're going to jump right into this thing. Buckle up! It's a heck of a journey....

WAKE UP CALL

My phone began to vibrate in my pants pocket...It was a cool night. There I was, alone. Standing in front of collegiate square. I didn't have the phone number saved but I recognized the area code. Reluctantly, I answered. Gathering as much composure as I could; offering a stiff

"hello."

A deep somber voice on the other end that spoke steadily,

"Good evening George, I wanted to call and talk to you for a few minutes."

"Yes, sir?" I replied, not out of respect but out of guilt, I knew why he was calling.

"Well George, I have to be honest with you, I'm upset. I thought that you and my baby were just buddies I didn't know you guys were involved like this. I trusted you with my baby girl; you know how fragile she is."

After a pause he sighed deeply, I could feel the burden on his heart from eleven hundred miles away. Then he said something that shook the foundation of the fortress of cards I had been ruling over:

"Everything thing that I have worked for in the last 22-years, you took it all away from me. Now, I have to start all over."

Shame... Shame is all I could feel. I was floored. Overwhelmed by the realness of the moment, I searched desperately in my mind for something or someone else to blame. Then came a moment of silence...followed by a defeated "Good-bye".

This was not the first time in my life I was confronted by a man for the mistreatment of his daughter. Putting my phone back into my pocket, thinking... This is his youngest daughter, my best friend, an angel compared to the likes of me... I remember the very first night I met her like it was yesterday. It was in the fall of 07. She was with some friends. She didn't speak much at all. It wasn't until spring break of 09 that we really got tight. Dorm-less and in dire need of a place to stay, she politely offered her couch to me for the week. I gladly accepted. From there we grew to be virtually inseparable.

Everywhere I went, she was there with me, and where ever she was that's exactly where I wanted to be. There had never been a person who I enjoyed being with on any consistent basis more than I did with her. She became my refuge. Frequently, on nights after having sex with whichever girl I was in love with at the time, I would call her up because I never wanted to be alone.

She was always there for me. I had become addicted to the games, women and lust stories. She was there through it all. I could be completely honest with her and she never turned me away. That was admirable. There were nights when I would give her my keys and she would hide them, so I couldn't leave, which was a safeguard. We both knew I was going to gamble away the little bit of money I had or fill some young lady's head with lies about love and wanting to spend a lifetime together.

I used to come in early mornings from a long night. She would always cook me pancakes and sausage before she left for class or practice. Going to class wasn't really my thing. College seemed like a mouse trap to me. As time progressed I could feel the emotions starting to shift. It was becoming more than just an ordinary friendship. Maybe it had been more the entire time and I was just naïve to the facts. Purposely, I neglected to acknowledge what I was noticing because it was just not a good time. For years my other women had accused me of secretly loving her more than I loved them. Some even went as far as making claims of us being sexually active.

To which I always responded "we aren't having sex! (And we weren't at that time) She's like a sister to me." Telling them that she was like a sister to me wasn't my best lie, but it did buy me more time to play the friends with benefits game with all of them; which is merely consensual human extraction. When we went home for holidays that's when I really missed her. Night after night, long conversations like a middle school love story. I knew it was getting dangerous, but we love danger. It's intriguing. The friend in me wanted to warn her, but the animal inside just wouldn't allow me to do it.

When I returned home from France in the spring of 2011 I knew it was on. There was nothing to stop me from being the dog that she knew I was. One night while in the club, as we were celebrating my return home, I noticed she was a bit more territorial than usual. We had clubbed together many times before, so it's not like we were in unchartered territory. Not only that, but we danced together.

It was a mini *Freaknik* session. You know how you're dancing with a female and the vibe is telling you to grab her titties and reach for her coochie but you're nervous because you don't want to shoot an air ball this early in the game?! That is exactly where I was. When it was time to leave, she held my hand all the way to the car.

The sexual energy was there! No doubt about that, but I was nervous. As I drove us home, I tried to formulate any reason in my mind to help me NOT cross this line, but my underdeveloped sense of integrity was no defense for what was probably about to happen.

We slept together every night, so this too was no big deal for us. When she came out of the bathroom, I could see it all over her. She was ready!!! Her legs; caramel and rising for days... She had on these white shorts that were ironically covered with hearts. Her skin touched mine...it was over! The next morning when I left to go to work I received a text saying that last night was a mistake and that we needed to go back to being just friends, but I knew that was just gibberish. There was no going back for me. I was like a shark that smelled blood. Only one issue; it was the blood of my best friend.

After our second "accidental" encounter, I asked her was she sure this is what she wanted to do? She knew my past. She knew my current state and knew well that I had shown no signs of slowing down. Everything that we both had cherished for all those years, all the innocence and love; it was at stake. Once again, I asked,

"you sure this is what you want to do?"

She responded, "we'll be ok"

It was as if the switch went off! From that moment on she was no longer friend. She was "girlfriend, sex partner, and lover" and I could no longer be honest with her because it would have constricted my maneuverability. I have no clue why women want to save men. There is no amount of love you can give to a man that has no desire to change. I knew what was going to happen from the beginning. Instead of being a man and a true friend, I proceeded as if I really loved her and wanted a commitment. Almost! I almost convinced myself of it.

At this point in my life though, I was currently in love with two beautiful women, falling in love with a third, having sex with the third's friend, courting a freshman, and was fresh out of nasty breakups with two of my other women. Upset about the two I had just lost, I needed a quick rebound chick. There was also this delta I was involved with because I was still heartbroken after her line sister left me for another guy. I was fresh off my fourth and fifth abortions. I had no car at this point and I was a college student during a recession, so condoms certainly weren't a viable option.

Oh, and I was playing flag football, so I had to also give my undivided attention to that. A very busy man, but I felt like I was handling things pretty well all circumstances considered. Things between she and I went smoothly for a while. My lies really didn't feel like lies because I believe she understood that I wasn't committed. All this was doing was subverting all the history we'd built over the years. Our friendship was progressively diminishing. She was the epitome of womanhood and virtue in my eyes.

Virtually, the last true hope that there were women in the world who obey their parents, loved God and believed their bodies were too valuable for uncommitted sexual wear and tear. Which turned out not to be the case. I tried hard to justify in my mind the reasoning behind her choices. What was her source of hope??? The best I could come up with was that I was a challenge and an opportunity to show all the other women in my life that she had what it took to tame me.

Rational or not, the thought infuriated me. She of all people should have known better than to pull a stunt like this. As time progressed, so did the lies, the other women, the excuses and the sex. I was keeping everything under control and her obliged until *it* happened. Fearful of it all along! Despite my fearfulness, I had told myself that if it happened this time, I would man up and take care of my responsibilities. After all, I did love her more than I loved the other women.

After all, I did love her more than I loved the other women.

She was my best friend and a relatively great woman, certainly the best that I had ever found. I mean... Yeah, she was having sex with a guy who didn't fully respect her, but hey, that guy was me and I know how to respect a woman! Right now, I'm just enjoying my youth. Besides, it is not my responsibility to do anything she doesn't require of me, I was a gentleman and I refused to force my respect onto her! So, the situation didn't seem that bad in theory. The news was confirmed! Post-confirmation, everything changed. I had been here many times before. It was not my first rodeo. I knew exactly what needed to be done.

I mean...

Yea, she was having sex with a guy who didn't fully respect her, but hey, that guy was me and I know how to respect a woman! Right now, I'm just enjoying my youth.

Besides, it is not my responsibility to do anything she doesn't require of me, I was a gentleman and I refused to force my respect onto her!

So, the situation didn't seem that bad in theory.

The news was confirmed!

Post-confirmation, everything changed.

I had been here many times before. It was not my first rodeo. I knew exactly what needed to be done.

Following the procedure, I began to create enough space to make her feel alienated. Then once I knew she had nowhere else to turn I would come back like the snake that I was and give her my "abortion speech". I would always play on "life" and how a baby significantly decreased her chances to be the self-made mogul she truly wanted to be and that she deserved to be married first.

After giving my spill, I would smugly say "but the decision is yours, I support whatever you decide to do." Just hearing those words echo in my mind makes my skin crawl. When we were on our way to having the procedure done, I remember rejoicing in my mind. Dodging yet another bullet and preserving my "good character", because who would revere me after having a child out of wedlock?

The atmosphere inside the vehicle was stifling. My perspective on the matter was completely different from hers. She felt betrayed. I felt nothing. This was my modus operandi. Everything that I had warned her about in the beginning was no longer applicable.\Her heart was shattered. Her emotions were all over the place. I can only imagine the shame she felt when we walked into the building to put her name on the waiting list. There we sat quietly as we waited for her to be called back.

Observing the faces of all the young women there, I could distinguish that an abortion clinic was certainly not where they imagined being at this point in their lives. *(Thinking to myself...)* How had they gotten to this point? What lies, and empty promises did their men make to them? What tactics did he use to get her into this building? Or did they want to come themselves? It's amazing what things run through your mind while sitting in a room like that.

The thing that was irrationally incredible about me is that I truly believed I was a better man than all the other men there who were forcing or allowing their woman to have an abortion! I was just there doing my friend a favor by helping her pay for her abortion, that she decided to have.

Totally disassociated from the truth of the situation, I had conveniently vindicated myself from any subsequent blame or fault that may have tried to emerge. This was her choice. All I could do was support her. On the ride home, there was nothing but complete silence. It was uncomfortably loud and eerie. She didn't even join me in the front. She coiled up in a blanket in the back seat, covered her face and cried the entire trip home. I hadn't seen her dismayed like this since that day in the village when the doctor told her she would be out of competition for at least a year to rehab her severe injury. I was lost. Stuck somewhere between my own cold-hearted, self-preserving action and my loyalty to a friend that had been tried and true.

Weeks passed...we saw each other from time to time at best. I would stop by to say hey and see if she needed anything. She never asked me to stay, and I never offered. Why would I? There was no benefit for me. My friendly obligation had been fulfilled and I knew that sex wasn't an option. After some grueling weeks of tears and excruciating hardships, she finally emerged from her hole. A shell of the angel she once was, but emergent nonetheless. We probed and probed trying to recalibrate our relationship to see how we'd go forward from this point.

Due to her extremely reserved nature, like a brand-new puppy being allowed to play outdoors for the first time, she was obviously a little timid. Knowing that I wouldn't have any opportunities at sex this early in the game, I remained patient. The one thing that I knew for certain, was that she still loved me. Knowing this allowed me to put the ball in her court and leave it there. All I needed to do was provide a level of consistency that made her feel as if I respected her healing process. This ultimately would allow me to regain her trust.

It was proof that the comfort was being restored. Sure, I was a butt hole, but I was still human. Seeing her at peace made me feel good even though I knew I was going to ruin it again. Then one evening, I got my opportunity. We had just gotten back from a long day outing. It was summer time, so it was warm outside. I rarely take many showers throughout the course of the day, but I knew how much she hated being sweaty, so I got naked and offered for her to come join me in the shower. She adamantly declined at first but I'm very persistent. She could never say no to me. I played fairly while in the shower. It would have been foolish to act any differently. This was the first time she had exposed herself to me in a while, so I was extra careful not to be too assertive.

I knew that if she didn't get dressed before she came out of the bathroom like she always did in the beginning that I had a shot to spark a flame. Not a definite one, so I had to be sure to play my cards perfectly. When she came into the bedroom she sat on the bed for a while, watching me intently. She had this way of staring at me without ever blinking that would creep me out, to be honest. The only time she did it is when she seriously needed to gather and quickly process information. Sure, there was all the pain from the recent past and the tears that never seemed to stop, but this was our new moment. Besides, that was the past. This was now. (I imagine she was thinking something like...) He still cares for me. We were best friends for years.

I'm sure he didn't hurt me on purpose. He's still growing. Anyway, I need this. He knows me better than anyone else... Then I made my move. Her mind was already made up, but what's a show without drama? She opposed. Pushed my hands away, but then I kissed her a little sweeter than ever before, a little more alluring than any she had ever experienced from me. The resistance was gone. She was my woman, yet again. Even though things had started to get back to what I like to call normal, there was another issue that was on the horizon. The summer was nearly over. Graduation had come and gone, it was decision time. She was from a different part of the country than I was.

Honestly, I did not know what my life would be like without her. It was frightening to imagine. She had been everything for me. Cooked, cleaned, dear friend, lover, supporter, and my confidante. If I had been man enough I suppose I would have asked her to marry me. The time surely came as we both knew it would…. she left for home. It was awkward for a while. The only remedy I could think of was to find a woman to fill the void. That's exactly what I did, but it wasn't the same. No woman could compare, I knew that, but I was afraid of commitment. It seemed to be a crime against nature for me to be with one woman. A few months later, we had our first rendezvous since she departed. I was very excited to see her again and I tried my best to show it while simultaneously hiding my true agenda.

My other ole woman was going to be in town the exact same weekend, so I had already concocted a scheme to get away for a night to do what I thought I needed to do. My plan went into effect on day two. I was at one of my friend's apartments and I pretended to be sleep when "house bae" called to see why I hadn't come home. She tried several times, even sent me a text message assuring me that if I did not call her or come home that she was done with me and it was completely over.

I knew that as long as I didn't respond until the next day, I could blame it on sleep and discount it all as a childish overreaction on her behalf. I'd become masterful at making young women feel guilty about accusing me of wrongdoing when I was blatantly in the wrong. Now that I had gotten her out of the way I could go see my other lady and hit those little mocha buns. Once I got with her, we ended up driving around the city searching for a cheap hotel room.

We eventually found one, and the show started. Yes, I told her all the lies she needed to hear. I needed all of her! One thing about me: I GO BIG! We woke up the next morning, got dressed and headed out. Once I dropped her off and got back to my friend's apartment I called my lady and pretended that nothing had happened at all. I told her that my friend and I had talked all night and that I had fallen asleep...then I rushed over to her and pretended to be upset at the idiotic mistake I had made.

The only thing that would truly show how upset I was at missing her that night was having a passionate round of sex with her, so I did just that. It had only been a few hours since I had just had sex with my other woman and here I was again naked and unprotected. This was my life. I loved it! The plan was executed to absolute perfection. That afternoon, I drove her back to the airport and just like that she was gone again. I have not seen her face since that day.

If I had known she was never coming back, maybe I would've hugged her a little tighter that day. We talked on the phone every day, but the distance was very disenchanting. We progressively lost more interest, because neither of us wanted to live in the other's city. For me, I thought it would be an "out of sight, out of mind" thing. WRONG. She stayed on my mind...

I really wish I could see her again and hug her now. The old adage is so true: *"you don't miss your water until your well runs dry."* MY WELL WAS BONE DRY! The straw that eventually broke the camel's back was my trip to Atlanta for my 25th birthday. It had been a while since I had been down to see my main man Slow so that's what I tried to convince myself I was doing. In my heart, I knew the real reason I was going. I had an old fling that lived in Atlanta from my college days and I was going to entertain myself at her expense. She was cool with it though... So that is exactly what I did. We had a great time and sealed the deal with a passionate night of pushing. WE PUSHED IT REAL GOOD...

This was only the second girl I had been sexually involved with since the ridiculousness I pulled that morning before I dropped my lady off at the airport. Ironically, the first girl that I had sex with after that day and before this trip to Atlanta turned out to be my most recent girlfriend's best friend. Go figure.

After this night in Atlanta on December 28, 2012, I decided that I had had enough. I called my house bae on the phone the next day and told her everything.

For the first time in my adult life, there was a conviction on me for being a liar and a DOG. It was something I had never felt before. I was nervous and didn't really know how to word it all, so I did it the best way I knew how; cold and very untactful. I vaguely remember how she responded, but what I do remember vividly is the weight that was lifted off my chest. In that very moment, it was made clear to me how I was going to finally turn my entire life around.

Romans 8:28 (The Voice) says: *"We are confident that God is able to orchestrate everything to work toward something good and beautiful when we love Him and accept His invitation to live according to His plan."*

This scripture is so real. It truly defines the love that God has for us and it makes it very clear why He would send His only begotten son to die on the cross for our sins. One thing that I had to understand about this particular scripture was this: ***just because God has the power to make it good doesn't mean that we made good choices.*** It is foolish to act rashly simply because we know that God can make it good. Behind that kind of thinking is the implication that "if I try this, maybe I can produce a greater outcome for myself than God has for me." That is a lie.

Even guys like me have hope in Christ. We can find redemption if we choose to believe and repent of our foolish indiscretions. Idolatry and pride HAD

CONSUMED ME. The worst part is that I caused so many others to suffer from my choices. My punishment for all my sins: having to find my way back to love again. I understand the love of Christ and what it entails, but my heart has been divided into so many places I have a hard time discerning what is love and what is lust.

We are all sowers and we are all reapers. The harvest depends on the seed you plant. You will always get apples from an apple seed. God gave us the irrevocable gift of choice. What we will become. The people we will trust. The fun we choose to have. The relationships we build. And ultimately the people we want to love. That day on the way back from Atlanta, I chose to really position myself to give God a try... but before I did; I NEEDED TO KNOW THAT HE WAS REAL.

WE NEVER KNOW WHO IS WATCHING!

You know, so many people don't believe in miracles anymore. My journey has been a miracle. My friend Wild B, who was my college roommate, and witnessed many nights of sexual debauchery said it like this: *"George, to see where you have come from is nothing short of a miracle. You are proof that Christ changes the hearts of men. It is rare to see a transformation this radical. I am proud of you man, I'll be praying for you."*

One-day Wild B shocked me. Years after we left college he told me that I was the reason he began to believe in God. That's incredible!!!! Because I was a heathen in college. He told me it was my faith. He was intrigued by the way I believed and the confidence I had. We never know who's watching. And we never know which moments are going to impact the lives of those around us. Sure, Wild B was impacted positively, but what about all of those who didn't have the proximity that Wild B had, what do they think of me?

Chronicles of Love

Zora

There she was. Holding hands, skipping, literally skipping to class with her boyfriend. They looked so happy! I thought to myself "Damn… I want a girlfriend like her." We were in the sixth grade, but using vulgar language was very common amongst my friends. We were cool. Cool people cuss! Excuse me, "Bool people Buss" Shout out to Issa. I remember the very first day she spoke to me.

She was walking with Wanda and they were heading outside of the sixth-grade building. She didn't say much, neither did I. She was amazing! Her skin was gold. Bruh, it was gold. Trust me. Body was jumping out the gym! You didn't see booty like that coming from little Rutherfordton Elementary where I sat in class with all the smart white kids and worked out hard math problems.

I had never witnessed anything like Zora before. By the time we got to high school she was top five in our county and all surrounding counties. Perfect figure. Radiant smile. Titty power. Perfect amount of attitude. And them buns stayed poked out! She was light brown sugar. All except for her hair; she was a mixed girl that didn't get that mixed hair flavor.

In all fairness though this was not her fault, her mama was white; she didn't have much experience handling black hair. Despite this, she was still a 10.5 to me. Seventh grade was a different story. For some reason when we got to seventh-grade sex was the hugest deal. Excuse me for a moment, Zora...There was one white girl that I and my friends all liked. We used to try to finger her on the bus.

To us she was fine. We all liked her, and she liked us back. One day we decided to take a stroll to her house. Her parents were gone, and we were going to run a train on her. It sounded fun, but I had no clue how a train worked. I was only 12. I was the youngest of my friends, but they treated me like I was a big deal, so it was all good.

At the time, Harp seemed to be the only one sure of himself. Vel was the oldest and I being the youngest was just happy to be a part of the sex locomotion. In the country, you always respect your elders, so once we got there, Vel was going to be the first to go.

We were peeping through the crack in the door to see how everything was going. I'm not sure why Harp was looking, but I was trying to see if I could get a few pointers. I didn't have a clue about real live sex, I was a virgin and maybe you're thinking "Uh, you're a 12-year-old boy! you should be a virgin" but I am telling you, I was the last of a dying breed. When we were young virginity was like a sickness that everybody desperately wanted to be cured of. Besides the boys in Forest City started when they were like 9-10 years old, so we were already behind the eight ball. After about 8 minutes of deliberation about who would be on top Vel finally came out of the room and confessed that he couldn't get hard.

I was too prideful to ask what he meant by that, so I strutted into the room like I was Mr. Marcus, stripped down and pulled out my condom. It felt so cool pulling out my condom (smiley face). I sat it on my tip and rolled it about a quarter inch back, unfortunately, that was all I needed at the time. I mounted the bed and climbed in between her legs.

As I proceeded to insert myself, totally unsure of where it was supposed to go but I figured something magical would happen if I just pushed hard enough. To my surprise, she looked down and said, "It's soft!" Immediately, I knew what Vel was talking about! I jumped off the bed went back outside the room and proudly uttered "dang bruh! I couldn't get hard either."

Not getting hard was actually a relief for me. It saved me from the nerve induced coma that I had nearly slipped into! I wanted to go home!!! And shouldn't have been there in the first place, but my friends were there so I suffered through it. Once I came out of the room "we", (Vel and I), decided that it was time to go and the majority always ruled. So, we left. This was my first real sex attempt in life and it was a complete failure. From there, I tried to shy away from anything sexual. It made me nervous. I hated the pressure of it all.

(Back to Zora) One thing about Zora, she was very forward. Her aggressive nature was not very attractive to me then, but she was fine; and when a woman is fine you just deal with whatever she brings. Right?

When the 3:00 pm bell would ring for school to get out we would be running through the auditorium to head to the bus and she would stop me and show me her titties. (hahaha...titty is such a funny word) Her titties were nice. I think...they were the first live ones I had ever seen, but what was I supposed to do with titties in an auditorium? And the bus was about to leave?

I did what any other seventh-grade tit rookie would have done. I paid my respects for about 6 seconds and shot out the door to go catch the bus. The summer was vastly approaching, and the sexual pressures were at an all-time high. She constantly badgered me with proposals to "play with my dick" and questions like "how big is it?" No one including myself had ever intentionally played with it before; as far as size went, I had never been asked that question and to make matters worse I had no other seventh-grade penis to reference.

For a seventh grader, the size of the package is relative. I just want it to be bigger than a few other guys'. This became an early obsession. Every girl wanted a guy with a big one. As if we could have gone to China and bought it direct from the manufacturer. Sex was stressful. I was already growing weary of it and I hadn't even started.

Intently searching for a way out of all this mess, but not being able to find one. I was popular. Popularity is a prison. If anybody was having sex, the popular guy should have been having sex too. Then the day finally came. We were meeting to do it at the local park. Yes, the local park! Where else could a 13-year-old boy and 12-year-old girl go for their friends to witness them make the biggest mistake of their life? Once we got there, I found her, and we entered this old nasty abandoned concession stand.

She laid down on the dirty ground in her teal thong, a 12-year old in a thong. Imagine that! The good thing is that I did have a condom. It was blueberry flavored. I was hard this time. One order of blueberry cupcakes, coming right up! Eureka! I was actually having sex!!! It fell out like every other stroke; we continued this for maybe 5-8 minutes then decided enough was enough. There were no orgasms involved. Really, I just had to do enough to say I did it. After I and my boys left the park, I was proud of myself. More relieved than proud, but still proud. I had finally been cured. After the cure came the drama. Zora decided to write a letter to share our experience with her friends. Apparently, they were enjoying the juicy letter a little too much, so one of the teachers decided to come take a gander.

Next thing I know, I'm being called to the office and on my way, I ran into her mama...without any hesitation, she demanded: **"Is this true!"** Y'all already know me, I lied. Then she said this, and I still can see the passion in her eyes *"if you're man enough to screw her, you should be man enough to admit it!"*

Looking back, I wish I would have had the presence of mind to tell her: "Ma'am we didn't screw". I just poked my meat around a couple of times, that's all. That was the truth. This was a big deal for a while but eventually, it died down. After our epic fail, Zora and I didn't really communicate for a while. It was too awkward. After that day in the park, I didn't really care much for having sex anymore.

Time passed, and the awkwardness was diluted more with each coming year. In the 8th, 9th, and 10th grade everybody was talking about masturbating. I didn't know how to masturbate and didn't care to learn. Around about the 10th-grade summer, we started to really invest our time in pornography. A whole lot of porn!!!! It was hardcore too. Grown people stuff! We had dabbled with it before but not like this. This was an every day, every weekend sleepover with friends, porn fascination.

My desire for sex was back! This time I was determined to get it right. In all honesty, porn was sex education for us. By the time 10th grade summer came around (when I had my first orgasm via masturbation) I was a porn pundit. Then I got hooked up with Addy. She was my first sex partner since Zora. Believe it or not, it was harder for me to get to body number 2 than it was for number 1.

My first sexual encounter was so terrible that I never wanted to have sex anymore. The only reason I'm mentioning Addy is because she is the reason I'm so bold with my sexuality. She wanted to do it everywhere! Our first sexual encounter took place at a gospel play. She put her mouth on my private in the auditorium while my home boys watched out for me. There were two other attempts that took place at school. The first one happened in the boy's bathroom. We were trying to have sex before fourth period. Much to both of our surprise, Vel walked in and caught us!

The second, we barely escaped. The janitor had come into the bathroom, who ironically happened to be the preacher's wife of my former church. That would've been a shocker for all of us. She thought I was the best-behaved boy in Sunday School. Haha, praise the Lord. One-day Addy and her mother came to pick up me to hang out with her at their house.

We got to her house, entered through the front-side door. Walked through the kitchen, which was adjacent to the living room; it was broad daylight. Her mama was in the kitchen, one slight movement from being in plain sight. We had sex right there in the living room. Mama never bothered to look. I don't know if this made me feel invisible or what, but from this day forward I wasn't afraid to do it anywhere. Addy was my first pregnancy scare. We were breaking bread in the back seat of somebody's car one night and the condom broke without me knowing. I thought that the sex had just gotten really good. Looking back, it's kind of funny that there was a time actually a time when a pregnancy scared me.

Anyway… The time had finally come for me and Zora to rekindle our adolescent flame. She was thinking destiny, I was thinking redemption. We came on to each other very strongly. Night after night, constantly pounding. There was a span where we went every night for about two straight weeks. This was how we got down! We didn't go on dates or anything like that. We had sex! It was the classic star quarterback pretty cheer captain story that is so glamorized on television.

Although I don't think she was the captain, she was close enough. Everything was perfect. We were both as happy as two teenage lovers could be. But then I met Charlie and Gia. They didn't go to our high school. They attended other schools within the county. I wanted to be loyal to Zora, but it was time for me to spread my wings a bit. Besides, I was "THE" man; I could juggle multiple women and make them all happy. So, I did. Eventually, things started to fall apart. Zora was hearing rumors of rumors and I couldn't sustain the lies any longer. My body was taking a pounding too.

I hardly got any rest. And on top of all that I was a 3-sport sometimes 4-sport athlete. Heck, I was a Wendy's High School Heisman Nominee! I had a lot of obligations to fulfill. As my senior year was ending, Zora's time with me had been tapered to nearly nothing at all. When we would spend time together all she wanted to talk about was how I had betrayed her and lied to her. Sex was happening a lot less frequently too.

In the fall of 2006, I left for college. Zora stayed home, and we didn't communicate at all during my entire first year of school. I met a gorgeous chocolate young lady with long silky-smooth hair my very first day at college. I fell in love with her instantaneously. We were sitting in the auditorium at freshman orientation. I looked over at Scoop and said to him

"I'm going to marry her."

Turned out to be an exaggeration, but I believed it when I said it. Her name was Tai. We were together our entire first year of college. She was lying beside me the morning I missed the team bus to Georgia for our weekend baseball tournament. Which consequently lead to my being dismissed from the team and losing my scholarship!

When the following fall came, I had transferred to my new university and I received word from an old friend that Zora was now attending university not far from where I was. In some ways, it was like fate had brought us back together. She came up to visit me that November and everything was back like it used to be. We hung out, had sex, laughed, chilled with my friends, and I even took her to a party with me; our first date in a sense.

I talked a lot about how I was changed from high school and that I still loved her and that I was now ready to settle down. I thought it all sounded nice to her. The next morning though, she left, and I never really saw her from that point until we would go home for breaks. Things had gotten complicated. I was involved with other women and she was giving sex just as freely to other men as the women in my life were giving it to me. At least that's how I felt. I don't know how true it was. More frustrating was that she didn't just accept my words anymore. She wanted action, which was something that I didn't really have time to give.

This episode continued year after year. There was always this hope in her heart that we would get back together. She earnestly believed that all roads would lead us to holy matrimony. I had a similar thought, but my reasoning was totally different. I always knew that if I could never find another woman who loved me and knew me well, I could always count on Zora no matter what I had done, and she would love me like none other. She was my "marriage insurance".

A couple of years later, in November during Thanksgiving break of my final year of college, I was back at home in Rutherfordton and I received a phone call. It was Zora. She told me she was in town and that she was coming over. When she got there, I opened up to her rather quickly and started to express to her the understanding that I have gained over the years through all the lies, sex and scandal. I expressed to her that I had found a young lady named Riley. I told her all about Riley, how brilliant she was and that she loved me about as much as she did. When I finished describing her, she looked up at me and asked me

"George, when are you going to grow up? She sounds like an amazing woman. I can tell that you care for her."

The only thing I could say was:

"I know she is the one. I'm going to ruin it though because I'm not ready for a love like hers."

There I was, sitting with the love of my life discussing the love of my life. It was confusing, and to make matters worse I wanted to have sex. We finally wrapped up the conversation. No true conclusion, just more loose ends. Unresolved emotions were the life force of our entire relationship.

Finally, in July (2012) as I was driving on the interstate I gave Zora a call and after 12 years of back and forth, love and hate, laughter and tears, joy and confusion we got closure. We both expressed the fact that what we were doing was unhealthy and it ultimately crippled our ability to love anyone else. It was amazing how relieving the mere concept of closure was and to hear the words eased my heart and soul. I was being healed, I could feel it. What does it mean to be healed?

Charlie

She had an amazing white peachy flesh that was alluring, to say the least. Much like the tree in Eden, her fruit was forbidden but very attractive. I remember the first time I saw her brown eyes and witnessed her smile. She stood about 5 feet 6 inches with an athletic build. Her rhythm was impeccable. A simple beauty, short fingernails that always looked freshly bitten, denim jeans and a typical Aeropostale blouse. It was her personality that made her so conspicuous.

The very first night we hung out was at a party in Golden Valley. A place black people aren't particularly welcomed, but you can slide through if you are with the right people. I was not a big partier, but I would go from time to time if there was a potential score afoot. After this first party, the heat was on! A few nights later she invited me to come hang out at some house that she and her friends frequently visited. Which was amazing to me! Who had a whole house that actually worked just sitting around with no one living in it???

We lived in our house. As did everyone else I knew. There were no extra houses. This was the night that truly exposed me to a new world of addiction. When we got inside, we hung around in the living room for a few moments with everybody, talking and laughing about things that were truly irrelevant to everyone's agenda. Then we finally got up and went to the back room. I was nervous as a mug!

She was only my third sex partner... (well, that's if you don't count Jamie. And I don't. Nothing really happened with her because we didn't know what we were doing. SMH! Ok... I should just tell this story. You know how they always say if you get caught too many times then you should stop doing it? Well, I truly failed my way to sexual success. I have been caught so many times in my adolescence: once by Zora's mama, Zora's aunt, by Jamie's mama, by the cops, by my mama, by my cousins, by my sister, and by my homeboys in the school restrooms. It never occurred to me or anyone around me that I might have a dang problem. But God has a plan. Because if he didn't I'd be dead from all the foolish stunts I've pulled to get some Wonton soup.)

*back to the story

...and moreover, she was the first white girl I would ever have sex with. There were three of us in the room. Me, her and her friend.

I began taking off my clothes and they complimented my body. Ayyyye!!! Confidence went way high after hearing that. Before I got onto the bed I pulled out the condom. It was a magnum, in the gold wrapper. They were the Rolls Royce of condoms then. If you could wear one of those you were legitimate. And being dick-legit is a big deal to a 17-year-old. Needless to say, I was proud of myself for that, I had come a long way from the days me, Vel, and Jet would walk to the gas station to buy $0.75 condoms and pretend that they were too small after we tried them on in the bathroom stall. As I began to take it out of the wrapper Charlie looked at me with an obvious inquisitiveness, so I asked,

"what's the matter?" In utter disbelief, she said "You use condoms George Hines? We don't use those..."

Now I must be honest with you, this was the moment I began to fall in love with this girl. Not because what she was suggesting was good. It was just daring! I was enthralled! Prior to this moment, I had always at least attempted to use a condom. We thought condoms were cool. Not because it showed we were responsible, but because it was evidence that we were having sex or at least were contemplating.

Almost naturally, I tossed the condom to the side, climbed unto the bed and we started having sex. (well actually that's a lie. I couldn't get hard due to an extreme amount of nervousness. Luckily her friend was there to give me some head to jump start us!) No foreplay, no concerted effort to arouse her or anything just a straight shot of raw sex. It ended quickly. Super quick! I honestly didn't know whether to be embarrassed or excited. Sex without a condom was the best and worst thing that ever happened to me.

It was the best because it was an indescribable feeling of pleasure. No condom really induces optimization. It felt better. My stroke seemed longer, and she seemed to enjoy it a lot more than any of the other girls ever had. Maybe it was because she was white? Either way, after this night I never viewed sex the same. From this point forward, no matter where I went condoms were the enemy.

Whenever I met a new woman, I would offer to use them initially, if she made me. I did this only to make it seem like I wasn't completely irresponsible but once

I had proven that, the rubbers were marginalized to moral support and ultimately neglected altogether.

After that night, Charlie and I were virtually inseparable our entire senior year of high school. Except for when I spent time with Zora or Gia, (Gia was my girlfriend during my senior year of high school. She was gorgeous). Charlie and I continued to throw all caution to the wind and fully indulge ourselves in the pleasure driven relationship that thrived through our final year of high school.

As we approached graduation and our final summer before leaving for college things became tough for us. She was heartbroken by the thought of not being with me anymore. She would cry night after night and I tried my best to assure her that things would never change. On occasion, I would even go as far to say that I was going to marry her and that everything she was worrying about would be laughable in a few years. We always dreamed of having a huge house in the country and a pearl white Range Rover.

Right before the summer ended, as we were preparing to depart for college, my life changed drastically in two phases: first off, I became brothers with a soldier from across town. He went to the same high school as Charlie. We were chilling outside in front of my house talking, sharing stories and everything clicked! From that night alone, we have blossomed into a synergy.

He is the man that I want to fight my battles with; he is the man I would die with. There has never been a question about his character or integrity. He is the man that taught me loyalty. He showed me how to persevere through an inexorable storm. If it had not been for him, these thoughts would have never existed in my mind.

Secondly, Charlie was pregnant. Prior to this, I had the one pregnancy scare, but this was the real deal. The very first thing you think about when you get a girl pregnant is the embarrassment from having to tell your parents and then the exaggerative thought that "my life is over!" I knew for a fact that I was not ready for a baby, neither was Charlie. The next thing I needed to do was figure how I could sell abortion to her and not make her feel like I didn't care for her. I knew I had two very strong forces working in my favor: her parents and our future.

Her parents, especially her father was totally opposed to her being with a black guy. That was a very big deal, especially at the tender age of 18. Even larger than that was the extravagant lifestyle and marriage that we had planned on sharing together. This type of hit would have certainly disrupted those plans. These two factors were enough to swing things in the direction I had hoped they would go in. Truthfully, it required very little convincing. She shared my sentiment. There wasn't any resistance. We had seemingly made the first executive decision within our relationship.

I remember leaving school that Friday to go be with her, the procedure was set to take place on the following morning. Once there, I scoped out the scenery, stayed and hung for a while then I left to see a few of my friends who also attended the same university. As I was making my rounds I decided to give Gia a call. She didn't stay far from Charlie. I walked over to see her, we had our usual round of hokey pokey, then I, with my faulty perception of manhood returned to Charlie's dorm room feeling accomplished for the night.

Here I was on the verge of penetrating Charlie, less than 4 hours ago I had been lying with Gia. Sure, I was an animal. Yea, it was nasty, but I loved every bit of it. Young wild and "free" but that wasn't what I loved most. I loved the control. I loved the fact that I was the manipulator, and everyone marched to the beat of my drum. The thrill of knowing something that neither Charlie nor Gia knew was the stimulation that was so riveting in my mind. I was completely hooked!

That next morning, we woke up and departed for the clinic. There was an unusual silence in the car. We were usually singing along with Chris Brown or Neo. She loved CB. I attempted to lighten the mood with some crude humor but to no avail. She didn't even acknowledge it. As we were pulling in, there were these protesters standing out front with signs of fetuses and they were screaming.

"Please, give this child a chance to live!"

"Is this what God would want for the child!"

It was a little demoralizing hearing those people say all those things. Although these were questions that I had already expressed inwardly, nonetheless we went forward. As we walked into the clinic, we were engulfed by a truly serene environment with melodic sounds to drown out the conscience screaming loudly within. It was almost as if the music induced hypnosis, helping make a totally evil act feel not as poignant. I sat quietly in the lobby as they called her name. I'd like to think that I kissed her and told her that I loved her as she went back, but I honestly cannot recall.

Sitting still for a couple of hours, watching intently as all the other young women cried tears of what could have been regret, pain, betrayal, discomfort or even dismay, but I was certain that none of them were tears of triumph or joy. I heard the door opening again, this time it was Charlie. Her face emotionless, her eyes had this emptiness in them that I cannot even begin to explain. I didn't know whether to hold her hand or get the door for her.

Once we got to the car and headed back toward campus, she asked me if I was hungry. Imagine that...of all the things she could have said, this is what came from her mouth. In this moment, I understood why it is that some black men cherish the companion of white women so much. I didn't have the perspective or facts to validate my thoughts then, but I have them now. (My aunt, who proofread this for me, commented: *"because they make no demands of you to be a better man!"* Now, I'm not sure how any other interracial relationships are, but this was certainly true for our relationship. Charlie demanded nothing from me. Ever!)

White women truly handle issues differently. I'm sure I am over-generalizing, but my perspective came by way of experience. It could be a cultural thing, but the mindset of white women differs completely from the mindset of black women. There was no way any young black woman I knew would have been thinking of my needs in this situation. Not that any one of them should have. That is not at all what I'm suggesting.

As life would have it, I was able eventually able to verify my claim. Charlie and I bounced back strong from this minor setback. In a relatively short amount of time, we were back kicking it just like we used to. I didn't mention this before, but I will now. Charlie had a lot of money! What she had she enjoyed spending on me. As I mentioned earlier, I ended up having to transfer schools due to some academic and athletic complications. It was her concerted efforts and finances that made the transition possible; on so many levels.

When I arrived at North Carolina A&T, I had only two pairs of shoes and just a couple of outfits. By the end of my first year, I had 15 pairs of shoes and more clothes than I could fit into my closet. It was all because of her.

She was the most valuable asset in my life. At this point in the relationship, we had already executed our second abortion and honestly, for me, it was painless.

I didn't even go to the clinic with her this time. I just told my homeboy to be sure she had it taken care of. Everything was great in my eyes. I had an endless supply of money, I was the starting center fielder on a Division 1 baseball team, I had the coolest and prettiest friends on campus. Moreover, I had accumulated a rack of coochie in a short amount of time and had no commitments. I WAS LIVING THE DREAM!

I did what I wanted to do, and I thought this meant that I was free. It felt like I was above reproach. Dudes respected me, more and more women wanted me! Who wouldn't want this life? Later in the first semester, one of my pretty friends and I became very close. Dangerously close from Charlie's perspective.

I assured her it was just a friendship and that she had nothing to worry about at all. I wasn't completely sure but I kind of knew it was a little more serious than I had led Charlie to believe. One weekend Charlie and her friend came up to visit me. By this time, I was tripping and not being considerate. The most thoughtless and disrespectful thing I could have done, I ended up doing... I made Charlie sleep on the couch while the girl she knew was creeping in on her was sound asleep in my bed. In hopes to ease the blow, I slept on the couch with her, but I don't think it made her feel any better. That next morning Charlie and her friend got up and left. The distance between Charlie and me continued to widen. I understood why, but I still pretended not to when we would talk to each other.

Prior to this encounter, I remember Charlie saying to me *"I don't care what you do to me, as long as you just call me and talk to me and tell me you love me I'll never leave you."*

When she said that to me, she had reached a point that was so low that she had totally dismissed her value and just wanted any level of attention I'd offer. I had totally crossed the line this time, but it's hard to let go of three years of history with a guy. Especially with all she had invested in me.

We talked on and off for a while. She questioned deeper about my relationship with Porsha and as usual, I promised her that it was merely a fling and that it wouldn't last very long. She quaintly accepted it for what it was. She even came to my game when we played against her university but the chemistry we shared had flatlined by now.

Eventually, it all just faded away and what was once the highlight of my life had been condensed to a mere story of a girl I used to know.

Porsha

The night I met Porsha we were all hanging out outside of the village. She seemed pretty cool then, but nothing about her was extravagant. No features stood out, and for some reason, she never ever did anything to her hair. It was all over the place, all the time.

Surprisingly enough, that was one of the most intriguing things about her to me. One thing I did notice though was that she talked a lot. She was always sure to let everyone know that she knew something about everything, but it wasn't overbearing. One Saturday Slow, Bad Burt, and I were walking to the football game. We passed by her without even recognizing it was her!

That was the first time we had ever seen her lavish, and to all our surprise, she was quite easy on the eyes.

One night, sometime after that day, were sitting in the room and she was speaking of a guy that had been pursuing her adamantly; the gentleman she was speaking of was a well-known figure in the sports world at the time. Her epic tale provoked me to say, *"well if all of those guys want you that bad I guess I should want you too!"* It's true.

To us, Porsha was just an ordinary girl, but she was a smooth operator, always in the right place at the right time. Porsha and I got very close. She stayed with us often. Like every night. The nights she didn't stay I rarely stayed. Porsha knew about Charlie, she knew about Bella, and all the others but it didn't faze her any. It shouldn't have, we were only friends at the time, but I believe everyone could see the storm brewing. Porsha and I welcomed it. It was intriguing and new. And it *felt* so right.

One evening, not special in any way. Porsha sent me a text that read "tonight I want you to rub my legs, they are sore." Even now, six years later I am still aroused by the thought of it. At this point in my life, I had been with several women, there were many encounters, many late-night messages, but this was the apex.

Porsha was and to this day, is the most riveting encounter my heart has ever experienced. To touch her was everything. I wish I had been disciplined enough to stop ensuing indulgence, but my young hormones were primed; there was no turning back. That night was a turning point in my life. There wasn't a greater sexual conquest for me. Porsha was IT.

It was the beginning of baseball season. I had broken a bone in my right hand which required surgery and removal of my hamate. Before, during and after my surgery, Porsha was right there. She even allowed my parents to stay over and watch after me the night I had the surgery. She was so bomb to me. I missed out on nearly the entire season due to my injury, which resulted in a lot of time spent with my friends and more over time with Porsha. It was marvelous!

When spring break came I had to be out of the dorms, but I was still able to travel with the team. So naturally, I stayed with Porsha at her apartment. I won't detail it, but it was an awesome week for us both. Not that we had any doubts before, but undoubtedly! After this week, we were in love.

The summer came quickly. It was time for me to head home. On the day I left her, it was terribly difficult. I was so captivated by her beauty. She was me. She stood right there in the doorway with tears in her eyes, one farewell hug after another until I finally ran off. Looking back at the memory of that moment...it was almost as if our souls knew that we should've just run away together.

Our lives were perfect in that moment. Perfect moments are so rare. They're unforgettable. Without much growth, understanding, and surrender; they're "ungetoverable" *(word I just made up meaning: impossible to get over)*. They can easily become the bane of your existence. For me, that's exactly what it became. This moment was as high as I had ever been.

Porsha's apartment lease wouldn't be up until the end of the summer, so she still had a couple of months to be in the city before she was able to head home for her short summer break. I was only able to see her sparingly since I had gone back home but whenever I could I certainly was amped for it. The final time I saw her before she departed was the straw that broke the camel's back.

To be direct, Porsha's parents were not fans of mine at the time. I couldn't understand it then but looking back I clearly see why they thought us being together wasn't truly advantageous for her. I was young, seemingly arrogant, brash, and unrefined. Though I was gifted, that was certainly not enough to win her parents over. Besides, this was their baby girl. They had set high standards and had exceedingly high expectations for her.

When I arrived in Greensboro for our final summer farewell, I was in for a pleasant surprise. Porsha's aunt was there. She had come up to help them pack up and drive back home. I wasn't aware that her aunt was going to be there, but I knew that didn't matter once her aunt finally realized that I wasn't just stopping by to say hello; I was staying all night. And not only that… I was sleeping in the same bed as Porsha. This was not acceptable by any means and I was starkly aware of that, but I was in a bind. I had gotten dropped off, so I had no ride.

Furthermore, I had nowhere else to go! I was nearly three hours from home. Adding insult to injury, her little cousins were there too. They occupied the living room space, so sleeping on the couch wasn't an option. It was a perfect storm. Even though the circumstances were dire; everyone tried their best to sustain an optimistic outlook. Her aunt put forth much effort to be cordial with me. The tension was heavy, but we pressed on until finally, her aunt called Porsha and me into the room to have a serious talk with us. She began to ask some truly penetrating questions that I honestly had never given serious thought to. Questions such as:

"Are you willing to die for my niece?"

"Do you plan on marrying her?"

Among others…but honestly, I was done taking her seriously after she'd asked about dying for her. I was a 20-year-old cock-smith. There were 100 women that I still needed to have sex with. So, all that she was suggesting seemed a bit extreme to me in the moment. My abrupt response of "No!" was more of a reflex than an anything else. The interrogation ended without a true resolve, but one thing I knew was that auntie did not approve of me, my responses, or my demeanor. I can only imagine the impact all of this was having on Porsha.

When I woke the next morning, I called my cousin to come pick me up and we left as soon as we possibly could. I kissed Porsha good-bye and gave a half-hearted salutation to her family before dearly departing. That same day I had left from Porsha, I received a phone call from her father. We had spoken a couple of times before. I truly respected the fact that her father was interested in knowing the man that his daughter was involved with. This conversation was different though.

He had not called to shoot the breeze or be cordial; he was calling to get answers to why I felt so comfortable disrespecting his baby girl and sister-in-law the night before. He was displeased. I understood why. What he had neglected though was the fact that I had been blindsided as well, but there was no way I was going to put the blame on Porsha. After about seven minutes of what seemed to be scolding, I had had enough. I interjected. In the most respectful tone I could conjure up I said,

"Sir, I totally understand where you are coming from, but the truth of the entire matter is that you are not my daddy. He doesn't even speak to me the way

you're talking to me now. I apologize for the way you feel but my intention was never to disrespect anyone. I thank you for calling but I'm done."

That ended the conversation and all but ended my relationship too.

The most shocking part is that I, with all my heart thought that I was justified in saying what I said. I wasn't. Not only that! I had idiotically disregarded the most obvious fact: she was his daughter! He had every right to call and inquire in whatever tone he chose to utilize. I wanted to be with her! That was virtually impossible without his approval. The summer was a rough and trying time for us both. Porsha was in pain and I couldn't be there for her like she was for me. We were in an awkward fix. She was attempting to love me while honoring her parents' wishes of focusing her energy elsewhere.

When we returned for the fall semester, things were ok for a short amount of time, but I could tell the dynamics had essentially changed. We had a conversation one day before an athletic meeting and she said to me that we needed to relax a bit...that some of the things we were doing we really didn't need to be doing anyway. I reluctantly agreed. She was right. Besides, I would have given or done anything to keep her close to me.

More time elapsed and things got progressively stranger between us. I was hearing rumors about a new guy that she was dealing with. He was older and in her eyes a bit more refined than me. I found out who the nigga was. The part that pissed me off was that I had been dapping dude up every time I passed him. I thought he was good people. He could've been. But that didn't matter now! He was trying to stick his yellow peter in my girl.

For the very first time in my life, I didn't feel like I was the man. It's a feeling that is hard to explain, not because I don't have the words, but because it makes me feel so inferior that I become dejected. That's the thing about love. People say that time heals everything, but they never say how much time.

Even though I was hurting and embarrassed, I knew that I couldn't lose my cool, so I stayed cool. Watching helplessly... and the night would have passed quietly had it not been for my brother. You see, he's not one for disrespect on any level. All he knew was that I was upset because in my mind Porsha was my woman. That was enough for the ensuing riot. I won't call it a fight because of the staggering odds; I'll just say it was a blessing that we both got out unharmed. What I understood about the whole ordeal was: no matter what went down, or why, it would have been said that I was fighting over a woman.

George Hines Jr. was way too cool for that. In my heart, I believed that any woman that I had to fight for wasn't an investment that I needed to make. In other words, "I don't fight over no woman. If anything, they'll fight over me!" Never considering that pride and haughty thinking dominated my entire philosophy. Entitlement was a stronghold.

Looking back, it was necessary that I be humbled, but I hated every moment of it. I was blinded and unaware of how much I had fallen for this girl. That night crushed every ounce of pride I had in me. It also created a monster of a man that vowed solemnly to never allow any woman to get close enough to hurt me again. For the next several weeks of my life, I just sat quietly in my dorm room. Seriously contemplating taking a life; his or mine. Didn't matter to me. The only thing that stopped me was the shame it would have caused my pops. I wanted his life to make her suffer, and I wanted mine because I couldn't control these candy ass emotions. Once the heart has been unleashed, taming it is nearly impossible. I tried earnestly to hate her.

Desperate were my attempts to stop thinking about her, but I couldn't. Up until that point in my life, everything that I touched, I mastered. Not being in control nearly drove me crazy. I was too stubborn to forgive, I was too vengeful to forget and too arrogant to show my friends I was bothered by it all, even though they knew.

Everything we go through in life prepares us for the moments that come to test us. If it had not been for the years of conditioning from my pops, uncles, and cousins reminding me that I was the man and I could have as many women as I desired to have; I truly believe I would have slipped into a state of depression. So, I gathered myself, connected with my main man Randy who was going through a similar situation and we started from scratch.

It's amazing how God grants favor to us even when we don't deserve it. Truthfully, if Randy had not been there for me that year I probably would've just quit on everything. I couldn't hit a baseball to save my life that year. And on top of that, I had an HIV scare, which I must add is totally different from a pregnancy scare. At some point in your life, a kid would make you smile or feel proud. I doubt that would ever happen with HIV. I could go on forever about Porsha.

She is the soul tie that I never can seem to untie. The way she spoke to me reminded me of the comforts my mama used to give me on those rough nights when my mind wandered off to dark confusing places. She would bring peace to my unsettled heart.

Even now (five years hence), I still feel that Porsha and I had a matchless connection. The energy we shared was astounding, and still illuminates us both when we reconnect. Some days I wish everything could be perfect again, but other days I couldn't care less. My propensity to indifference is my biggest inconsistency. It induces much carelessness, procrastination, and ultimately makes me distastefully unaffectionate.

After it all went down, Porsha said to me

"George, what was I supposed to do? My parents thought that I had

lost my freaking mind! I thought you were going to fix it. You always fixed everything."

Well...this was beyond my level of "fix-ability"; only Felix could fix the situation we had gotten ourselves into and he was nowhere to be found. Consequently, we set our emotional sails and allowed the wind to blow us wherever it willed.

BELLA

It was a Saturday in early September, close to her birthday; although I didn't know this at the time. The first thing I noticed about her was her ashy elbows. She had clearly neglected to grease that day, or maybe she had missed a spot. Aside from the ashiness, she was radiant!

Her hair was like the finest woven silk. She had a classic almond tone that ran deep into her soul. She was athletically slim, slim-thick is what they call it now and very energetic. I liked her. I knew she would like me too if I ever could find the right opportunity to make my move. Weeks passed; I was an intently observant young man, always looking for clues and opportunities to catch her eye.

I could never seem to get the right angle on her though. She was always with friends. I knew that would not work, she had the pretty friends that seemed to love to make a guy feel unworthy of their time, so I had to find a more favorable alternative.

Then I found it! There was a guy in my analytical reasoning class. He was gay, but he hadn't fully accepted it yet. He was good friends with her at that time. I knew it would be super easy to communicate with him. Once he thought I was cool it was on to the introducing phase which worked majestically.

We were leaving the cafe one afternoon and he introduced us as we were walking down the steps. She was intriguing, to say the least. I loved how comfortable she was with meeting me the first time. Not wanting to be too aggressive, I softly corralled her hand to exude my gentleness. She was delicate. I wanted her to know that I knew it. We began to hang out. She turned out to be much more fun than I had anticipated. It was going great, and I was in no hurry to make any moves.

By this time in my life, I considered myself a sexual genius, but sex was never my only goal. I genuinely loved getting to know people and who better to get to know than a woman who you want to have sex with? It seemed radically logical to me. Bella and I were practically together from the fall of 2007 until this past fall of 2013. She and Riley (you're going to get to know Riley later) literally witnessed it all. The only distinction between the two was that Riley got the truth from me, while Bella had to use intuition and piece things together on her own.

Shortly after Bella and I began warming up is when I met Remy, who was introduced to me by Porsha. In my eyes, Remy and Bella were the complete supplementations to create the perfect woman. Remy was flawless in appearance. Her body had more curves than a rollercoaster. She was very outspoken. She was sexy. She needed attention. More than anything she loved sex. I loved her too. Remy was everything that Bella was not. I learned to appreciate them as individuals. Moreover, I got what needed from them both.

Bella never complained much about anything. The turning point in our relationship was the night she came into the village (my dorm room). She had apparently gotten a hold of one too many drinks at the party. She needed to talk to me. I couldn't invite her in to my suite because Porsha was there with me and Slow hanging out like she always did back then. I hated a drunken woman more than anything on the face of the earth, but I went out to listen to what she felt she needed to say to me. She was completely open.

This was a side I had never witnessed from her. She told me that she was really feeling me and that she felt our relationship could be awesome if I would just give us a legitimate chance. Then she said the magic words: **"The sex is good! You don't even have to worry about that."** After this conversation things went to another level.

For the entire first year of our relationship, we were extremely happy, but there was so much that she had no clue about. She had no clue that Remy and I were spending just as much time together and I was telling her all the same love stories. She didn't know that I was having unprotected sex with Remy, and to make matters worse my friendship with Porsha was evolving more each day. Despite all of that going on, Bella and I were still thriving in my mind as well as in hers.

As time progressed Porsha exploded onto the scene and became the only priority. Bella never complained. Remy, on the other hand, hated Porsha. To her, it was the ultimate disrespect. After all, it was Porsha that had introduced us. During it all, Bella still came around when she could. We spent many nights together and I would assure her that the time I was away from her that I was focusing on baseball and I still loved her more than anyone else.

When the first year of school ended, I knew this was my grand opportunity to reestablish the broken trust between Bella and me. She lived relatively close to me; especially in comparison to the others. My brother Stack would drive me to her house, so we could chill. We never went anywhere or did anything special; it was just the fact of me traveling that made everything seem genuine.

By the time we had returned to school for our second-year things had drastically changed. My main man Slow, the glue that seemed to hold me and all my friends together had transferred to another school. One of our other good friends was pregnant so she had to leave school for a while. I had recently received news that a young lady I was involved with miscarried the baby she and I were having and to make matters worse I no longer had Charlie to support me financially.

The thing that bothered me the most about Bella was that she didn't feel compelled to act the way I wanted her to act. She didn't listen. I needed a certain level of control over my women or I just didn't feel like a man. This was a big problem for me. I tried various new approaches to mold her the way I needed to, but none seemed to do the trick. Time continued to pass as it always did. New women began to enter the picture. There was Jojo (you're going to meet her soon), and Riley, who grew to be my very best friend.

PSA: If at any point, you realize you're having a hard time keeping up, don't feel bad. This is my life and I struggle to keep up. I'm writing it to you just as it happened. All these relational encounters ran together in the exact way I'm presenting them to you. Cool? Cool.

Porsha was gone. She left after her sophomore year for another university. Her departure left a huge void that I desperately needed to be filled. This was Bella's chance to prove her value to me. That's exactly what she did. She showed me that even after all the known foolishness and my conscious decision to be with Porsha and neglect her wasn't enough to eradicate the love she had for me.

Sadly, it still wasn't enough. I continued to lie, cheat, and manipulate every chance I got. Throughout the whole relationship, I believed that in my heart I truly loved her. Convinced that my actions were just; because with all the wrong that I did there was still enough good for her to feel like she should have stayed. To me that was love. I knew I was out of control, but I was in too deep to get out. Truthfully, I didn't want out. I loved myself for what I was doing. I had grown to be my very own obsession.

Bella's senior year and the final semester before her graduation was the spring of 2011. I had left to play football in France that January and things between us were really complicated, to say the least. She knew about my relationship with Jojo. She knew about the time I spent with Jordan* and she was highly skeptical about my "friendship" with Riley. I hoped that this time apart from one another would allow a lot of my foolishness to fade into the background.

*(You won't meet Jordan. She was just an interim fling)

When I returned home, it was time for Bella's graduation. We hadn't communicated much while I was gone but it was enough to secure me an invitation to her graduation dinner.

Finally, after 4 years of waiting, I got to meet her family. Family was my forte, I could sell the "respectable young man" dream better than anybody. When I arrived at dinner I shook the hands of all the men and gave hugs to all the women. I took the initiative to pray for the food and I even stood before everyone and gave a graduation speech. The speech was awesome! I know what you're thinking... "what a butthole!" True. But you also must remember that Bella and I had spent a lot of time together. So, yea, maybe my character was off, but I knew her well.

This was exactly what I needed. After this, we were back at it like crack addicts. Things were clicking on all cylinders again. Now that the year had ended she was moving to another apartment complex. Neither of us had any money, so instead of calling two men and a truck, we utilized what we had: one man, a Kia Sephia, and Bella. We loaded it down and strapped the mattress to my hood. It was moments like these that I believe made her feel we had a future together. They even convinced me at times that we were destined to be together. The only problem for me was that I had experienced at least ten of these moments over the last couple of years with multiple women.

One night after leaving Bella's apartment, I doubled back to see a young lady that stayed in the very same apartment complex as she did, and I spent about two hours chilling with her. All I talked about the entire time was how different I was than all the other guys and that she needed a man like me in her life. I told her about all the things I had done wrong and how I had learned so much from my past. She was truly interested, and I was on fire. It went on for at least 45 minutes then I finally decided that I was satisfied with myself, so I digressed.

Before I left, I offered a proposition that I didn't think any woman would refuse...I asked her could I eat her right there on her couch before I left for the night. She laughed and said "What! Are you kidding me?" With a great deal of embarrassment and disappointment, I flippantly insisted that I was only joking, but I was as serious as a heart attack. No woman had ever said that before. I was shocked. As I walked to my car, I pulled out my cell phone and called my mama.

I said to her **"mama, I believe I have absolutely lost touch with reality."** It was true. I had.

The fall had returned. I was back to school finishing up my final two semesters. The "school" portion of college was dreadful. To help focus, I decided, along with my little cousin to get a one-bedroom apartment in hopes that it would settle me down and isolate me to focus on my life.

My apartment was nice. I soon realized that what I had originally planned as a responsibility escape would become a fiasco. Bella was an integral part of this fiasco. At this point, I needed to be sure I kept things cool between us. Not because I wanted things to be cool; I just didn't have a washer and dryer. She didn't have a car at the time, so this was our equal medium of exchange. To be sure that my taking never became too one-sided (this was a rational attempt in my mind to be fair. I was truly detached in this regard.

I could justify anything to make myself feel deserving of something that I hadn't merited).

After I had totaled my car in an accident on my way to Atlanta to check out my man Slow things got a bit more difficult for me. Now I no longer had a medium of exchange. No longer could I justify not calling, not spending time and not doing the things she truly cared about. She was so genuine. I remember one day we walked from her apartment all the way over to mine to hang out. She never complained or made me feel like I was less of a man for that. Even now, to this day it still touches my heart.

Something was changing in me. It was hard to explain then, but I could feel the shifting taking place. Things that never got to me were bothering me; I was more emotional about the simple things in life. It was as if I had received an epiphany in life and I did everything I could to keep it at bay. Things had changed for me. I was tired of running but running was all I had known. Gambling had lost its flavor, sex had become a job but "if a man doesn't work, he can't eat". I couldn't quit. Besides, I wanted to be the man. I wanted to be praised. I needed to feel important. George Hines Jr. was a big deal and I couldn't let go of that. It was all coming to a screeching halt. Homecoming of 2012 was our last passionate rendezvous.

Riley and I were an undisclosed item now and I no longer lived in Greensboro, so it was harder to maneuver. I knew this weekend was the optimal opportunity for me and Bella, but Riley had traveled a long way to see me. There was only one way to ditch Riley and though it was very unrefined I knew I had to do it. So, I did. After the game that evening we went separate ways. I knew she was going out to the club and since I didn't club I was able to structure the lie. When she had settled in for the night it was around 1 am, a prime time for me to say I was asleep without too much static because that could have certainly been the case

All I had to do was ignore her calls, and in the morning, I would just tell her I dozed off with my phone on silent. Now that everything was in place I had to see if Bella would even be game. I texted her...BINGO! It was on. I picked her up and we drove around for at least an hour searching for a hotel. We finally found one that wasn't booked. As we waited in the lobby for the room to be prepared she allowed me to hold her as we sat in the only available seat in the lobby.

In that moment we had totally disregarded all the past. Totally neglected all the hurt and the lies and we just lived for the moment. Almost as if we both knew this was it, this would be our final encounter.

Her image was vivid and stunning, to say the least. She was no longer the slim athletic young girl that I met with the ash on her elbows; she was a woman! Her legs were flawless, she was a baby stallion. Her hair still sparkled like the blood diamonds from Sierra Leone, her smile was endearing and our chemistry as vibrant as the royal blue dress that affectionately hugged her undeniable curves. She was magnificent. She was the sweetest taste of sin; living up to every word of the drunken promise she'd made me all those years ago that night in the village. Just like that, the sun was up and the magic we had passionately created was merely a memory. And...my last one-hundred dollars. Welp, time to call Riley...

Jojo

The first time I saw Jojo I knew we needed to be friends. It was a crisp sunny day in Aggie land and she was there with her teammates rocking the house like they always did. I told my roommate GG that she had to hook me up, and with little reluctance, she did just that. JoJo was different than any other women I have been involved with before. She was intriguing, and she was brilliant! She knew a lot about everything. She was girly, deceivingly sexy, and she was a tremendous amount of fun.

Naturally, it did not take us long at all to hit it off. I remember swinging by her room on random days and playing mahjong titans on her laptop, making small talk and laughing. When I met her, she was dating a guy that didn't deserve her; I didn't deserve her either, but I was infinitely cooler than that nigga was! That alone made this a lay-up. We would chat often about how badly he talked to her and how it made her feel worthless.

Jojo had a skin tone that I considered light skinned, but with a fluorescent undertone. She glowed like a sunflower all the time. She was the epitome of light.

We were like two foreign elements that had never been mixed but because of a few subtle similarities and many keen distinctions, the thought of mixing was provocative.

The night that I really realized how much I cared for Jojo, the team had traveled to Daytona Beach for our weekend series with Bethune-Cookman. The entire time we were gone she was the only thing on my mind. I couldn't wait to get back to her. After our 75-hour bus trip home, we finally arrived at about 4 am. She had waited up on me all night. Maaaaaan... I ate that cat and hit them buns until the sun came up!

Now, Jojo was certainly not a nag by any stretch of the imagination but even she would eventually grow weary with a relationship that had no boundaries. Instead of me trying to clean up my mess, I figured I could buy more time if I just expressed my pseudo-concern on the matter. So, that is exactly what I did. I explained to her that I understood that she deserved more and that more is exactly what she would get once she had completely removed all the ambiguity from her past relationship. She was diligent in that regard, but I, on the other hand, procrastinated, and eventually just pretended to have cut all ties around me.

As time progressed we continued to grow closer. One weekend, she invited me to come up and meet her family. I didn't necessarily like any of the food they had, but I ate what little bit I could stomach. The thing that caught my eye was the curiosity and genuine hospitality of the women in her family. I had asked my brother Trap to come along with me. Whenever you are not fully committed and need a second opinion, always take with you a diversion who's also able to help assess people and situations. Jojo sat us down at the table and politely served me first then my brother second. While we were eating, her aunt, who was sitting adjacent to me, asked me: **"are you a Christian?"** Amazed at her boldness and pleased by the question I chuckled my way into a smile and answered, **"yes ma'am, I'm a Christian."** And for as much as I understood about Christianity at the time, not only was I a Christian, Heaven was a sure thing! Glad I didn't die then...

Moments like this, at Jojo's dinner table, keep me connected to people. Not only am I connected through experiences we share; it is also hard for me to disassociate myself from the individual. To me, it almost seems unfair to keep the knowledge I gained from a woman and totally discard the woman. All this simply means is that once I get close to someone, I have a hard time of letting go of them because of the qualities I like about them. This causes me to end up holding on much longer than I should.

We continued to grow. Like was approaching "love" and love was driven more by passion than understanding. One night while riding with Bella back to her house I received a message from Jojo, in which she told me that she loved me. This was the first time she had ever said it to, and coincidentally Bella was right there staring at my screen, reading the message as I read it. Bella was livid. Little did she know, I was just as surprised by the text as she was.

There were two women that I was involved with that Jojo was openly disgusted by, and she expressed it to me often. Anything that she didn't like I tried hard to make her feel obliged. As I mentioned, we were not exclusive, well at least I wasn't, but she tolerated it. Jojo was a special woman. She was super intelligent and as I mentioned, her family was of the highest moral standard. I couldn't understand why she was so intrigued by me. It felt like I was a fantasy. I didn't want to be the charmer, although it came quite naturally.

Jojo and I continued speeding headlong down this sensational journey to nowhere and then the inevitable happened. She was pregnant. Here I was again, in a very familiar place. Not the least bit nervous or unsure of what my ensuing actions would be. I allowed Jojo to internalize the situation before I ever expressed my sentiments on the matter. Hearing how she expressed herself would allow me to devise a plan to effectively approach the situation to ensure my desired result. There were only a few things in my life that I was certain of when it came to my relationships, family, and children:

1. I didn't want to be with a woman who already had children.

2. I wanted my children to have the same mother.

3. Whoever I had my first child by was going to be with me. I would have done whatever I had to make the relationship work.

With those few certainties in mind, there were also some major reservations that were tied to them; because I knew I would ultimately work it out with whatever woman that had my first child I knew that put me in a box. There is nothing more detestable to me than being put in a situation where I feel like I do not have favorable options. This is the feeling that allowed me to perfect my *"abortion speech"*.

This was my fourth time being in this situation. Not all these situations called for the speech but there were three that certainly did, this was one of them! Once she had finally processed the entire situation and internalized all the circumstances and implications, it was time to deliver (no pun intended).

Whenever I would give this speech I would always position myself lower than the women. This was a subliminal indication given to express the power as well as authority they had in the moment. Ultimately allowing me to place the decision in their hands. This way, if or when it backfired, no one would be able to place the blame solely, or even partially, on me.

I would begin my monologue by stating that **"this is a situation of great magnitude that should not be taken lightly or expressed to many people. This is something that we should handle on our own and not weigh too heavily on the thoughts or opinions of others."** By saying this it gave a false sense of security that made her feel as if I was focused on our well-being and that I did not want anyone making or influencing a decision that would drastically impact our futures' not theirs.

The word "future" is operative. The implication behind that word, when added to the circumstances incubates the thought that "futures" could be altered radically.

Then I would go on to say: **"You are a brilliant young woman. You would be awesome with a child; there is no doubt about that. The biggest thing that concerns me is the fact that your life has to come to a complete stop! I must be honest with you, I still get to chase my**

dreams. You, on the other hand, get cheated out of the amazing opportunity you have before you, and I don't want you to hate me for that on down the road."

At this point, she is just looking for some type direction. (Even though I am the antagonist she can't see that. In moments of chaos it is human nature to search for any sign that makes you feel like things are normal again, even if they are not.) She is so emotional and in such a state of cerebral inebriation that she is absolutely suggestible. The power that she has in this moment is more than she desires of possess. At this point, I would transition myself to another part of the room (usually standing), to affirm my position as the "man" and to completely take dominion of the decision while allowing her to feel like it was still hers.

Finally, I would give my closing sentiments: **"There is no sense in compounding a tough situation. We have not reached a point where we are ready for marriage and you deserve better than to have a baby by a man out of wedlock. I am going to support you**

either way it goes; I just cannot live with the fact that everything you have worked for has to be thrown off to the side. You have sacrificed too much to get here. We have so much more time left, and more than anything else, I want you to be ok."
This was just a bunch of trash.

Trash that didn't do anything but confuse her more and force her back into the mindset of losing her future. Also, she now had wrapped her mind around the fact that keeping the baby paralyzed her dreams, youth, and fun. For me, it didn't change anything.

In a committed relationship with boundaries this may have sparked a different thought, but for a young educated college woman with massive standards and expectations from her friends and family these thoughts evoke a totally different feeling. Feelings like: you may miss out on something, you may disappoint someone you love, or feeling like you may lose some freedom today that you have grown accustomed to, creates pressure.

In a ditch effort to keep a "good life" from changing to a life with countless unknowns we will do almost anything. It is almost like we become a totally different person. The reason being is that in our hearts we believe that we are not the kind of person that would do gruesome things like have abortions or advocate abortions, but I have learned over the years that the human heart is radically depraved and will stop at nothing to realize self-preservation.

We went through with it. It devastated her. I witnessed an angel of light transform into a shadow of the woman she once was. Everything from this point on was downhill. We hung on for a while, we tried our best to rekindle the magic, but it just was not there any longer. There was only one final request from Jojo, **"just don't fall in love with Riley."** I have never been one who was good at keeping promises...Jojo was well aware of the friendship that Riley and I had. She was not fond of it at all. She warned me adamantly that Riley had intentions of being much more to me than just a friend. As turns out, Jojo's analysis was spot on.

Riley

And then there was Riley; the best woman I have ever known. We met Riley our first year at A&T. Ironically, she and Porsha knew each other well. Riley ended up being the woman of my prayers. She was perfect. She was pure.

Riley was the first woman I have ever met in my life that was still a virgin after the age of sixteen, and certainly the only female virgin that I had met in college. Truthfully, it made me question many things about the way she was raised. I was intrigued because I wanted my daughters to be like her. Riley was everything to me. She was my sister. She was my friend. I wanted to protect her like a daughter, I respected her like my mother, honored her like a grandmother, and spoke to her like a confidante.

If it weren't for my insatiable desire to conquer everything, Riley would have been my wife without any doubt. For years, I was able to keep my animal nature at bay, but it all changed a couple of weeks after I returned from France. I was lying in bed with Jojo and received a text that read: **"I want you to take my virginity..."** Then she followed up with an "April fools!!!" But she and I both knew that was far from a joke. This was the day the dam broke. All the inclinations and perversion I had managed to separate from our friendship I could no longer imprison. They were free and rampant. Frankly, there was nothing I could do to avert the imminent calamity.

Of course, it didn't happen immediately after receiving the message, but I believe we both knew it would only be a matter of time before the opportunity presented itself. Like clockwork, it came. One night she, I and a few of her friends decided to go to the club. We had been out together many times before, but this event was different. We danced with intent. It was not the cute playful dancing that friends do together. I could sense danger afoot. As we were walking to the car, she held my hand.

Our fingers were interlocked. And I knew tonight would probably be the night we cut ties with purity and started our inevitable plummet toward the all-consuming abyss that I call narcissism. I had been warned by my uncle that this was a line I certainly did not want to cross. His words to me were explicit:

"Nephew, once you hit the pussy, the friendship is over!" He had never in my
life given me advice about preserving a relationship with any of my women, but he offered this piece to me freely. I totally disregarded it, but he couldn't have been more accurate!

That night I showered and climbed into the bed as I normally did. Unsure how things would spark off or if they would at all, so I waited patiently. The last thing I needed was a false positive on my behalf that leads to an awkward situation with my best friend, who at the time was my supreme resource for survival.

Riley usually showered after me. When she came to bed it was usually basketball shorts and a T-shirt, but as you already know tonight was different. When the bathroom door swung open, what emerged may have been the most exquisite thing I have ever witnessed in life (hormones were in overdrive). She had on the smallest little heart shorts in the world and a tank top with no bra. Now, I'm no genius but 1+1 is 2! She was definitely about to throw that thang in a circle for your boy!

The next morning, I had to leave early for work. Of course, there were hints of regret, awkwardness, and remorse, but it was more formality than anything else. She needed to reiterate to me that this wasn't the way she operated because she was a lady and I needed to make an attempt at reestablishing the respect and reverence for her as a woman. The friendship didn't stand alone anymore. It was suddenly lost in a lustful escapade that we both wanted to transmute into love, but neither of us had the essentials. This night was the beginning of the end of a beautiful union.

My 7-year struggle

"Sometimes it takes 10 years to get that 1 year that will change your life." ~ Unknown

When I was 18 years old and sex had become a very integral portion of my life, I was totally out of control but like any other addict, I believed in my heart that I could stop this madness any day that I felt like it.

My mama challenged me.

She said, **"Son, I want you to sanctify yourself."**

I said, "what do you mean ma?"

Ma: **"I want you to take seven days and just take a break. No sex, no nothing for seven whole days."** It was ma, so of course, I said ok.

Saying ok was very easy, so was day one, and day two, but after that, it wasn't so easy. The closest I had ever come to completing the seven days was one the summer of 2010.

I was six days and some hours in. All I had to do was hold off until Remy and I returned from the movies. The seven days would've been complete. But by now, y'all know me; I couldn't hold off. She was looking too good to wait! Besides, I had next week.

Being rational has always been one of the key factors in my life and decision making. If I ever do something, it must make sense in my mind. Not having sex and jacking off were just two things that I could, under no circumstances rationalize. I thought that a man was supposed to have sex and orgasms as frequently as possible. And on top of that, I had at least 20 more hoes that I know for a fact needed this wood.

It wasn't until August of 2012 that I completed the seven days without sex, but even then, I still hadn't stopped masturbating. After a life-altering epiphany on December 29, 2012; the morning after my 25th birthday, I made up my mind that I was done having sex. I can't tell you what happened, but the thought of casual sex just left a bad taste in my mouth.

Ever had a favorite food or snack? And you eat it so much that it just becomes a staple in your appetite, but one day you get sick. It may have absolutely nothing to do with your favorite food, but the thought of eating that food makes you want to gag! That's what I was experiencing. A few short weeks later, on January 20, 2013, I totally committed to being abstinent. No more sex, no more masturbation. I wanted to truly be in fellowship with God.

I wanted God to tell me who I was so that I could become the man He created me to be and this was the promise I made: **"Lord if you will give**

me a chance to change my life, I will be truthful to as many young women as I can about saving themselves from guys such as myself."

On day 6, I was in the Marriot in Asheville and I was nervous. Only one day away from the goal. Grabbing my phone, I called Riley. She always made complex things so simple.

I told her how I was feeling, and that I didn't know what to do after day 7. Her response, **"Start back at day 1."** Suddenly, I had a new perspective on life and the rationale that I desperately desired so many years ago was ever present in that moment.

As time progressed, I wanted to know what was happening to me. An understanding was something I needed. If sex was no longer going to be a part of my life I needed something to take its place. So, I began with rationale. In my conscience, I could hear the voice of God so clearly. It was almost as if He wanted me to hear myself think. This is how it went:

God: **Do you love your mother?**

Me: Yes, I love her very much.

God: Do you love her more than you love me?

Me: Definitely not!

God: Well why do you never have sex or masturbate in your mother's presence, but you never hesitated to do either in mine?

Me: (complete silence)

This transformed my thinking! From this conception of thought, I could finally complete my seven-day sanctification and go so much further. Not only did God cover me through the seven days, he covered me from January 20, 2013, until February 9, 2014. Zero sexual activity. The purpose of that story was for this truth: **We have no power or knowledge to accomplish any righteous acts without acknowledging God.** After I hit the year mark I began to brag within my own heart, as well as bragging to others about what I had done.

I hadn't done anything. It was the spirit that watched and guided me, bringing all convictions back to my remembrance so that I wouldn't put myself in situations and fall back into temptation.

Luke 11:24-26

When the unclean spirit has gone out of a person, it roams through waterless places in search [of a place] of rest (release, refreshment, ease); and finding none it says, I will go back to my house from which I came.

And when it arrives, it finds [the place] swept and put in order and furnished and decorated.

And it goes and brings other spirits, seven [of them], more evil than itself, and they enter in, settle down, and dwell there; and the last state of that person is worse than the first.

These verses are the ones that came to mind when I first fell, and I realized how truly accurate they are. And by "fell" I mean: began having sex again.

There is this notion that men can have female friends and hang closely with them without any danger of sexual tensions emerging. That's just not true.

My desire for sex was tremendously greater than I remembered it being. Whenever this young lady and I got around each other it was over! There was one occasion where I had attempted to talk her down, talk myself down, and I even threatened to leave but when I tried, the pull was so strong that I ended up right back on top of her.

I had been deceived.

In my mind, I thought that it was me that had stayed clean for a year, I believed it was me that had accomplished this great feat. Worst of all, I was confessing that God did it when I had lost my ability to hear God's voice.

My testimony had become a trophy. One that I felt deserving of, but there is nothing we could ever do to deserve God's grace and mercy.

Here I was, committing the very sin that I speak so adamantly against. I was back being the same old George that I had always been; full of myself, manipulating, scheming, and fornicating.

The only difference: I couldn't find peace in it. It was forced, and I knew it. I was controlled by the sin nature and immediately after pleasure was the misery of disobedience.

To make matters worse, all this was happening with a young lady who had real respect for me. I was letting her down.

She hadn't fully realized the depths of her disappointment just yet because there is the emotional euphoria that blinds us from the truth, but it would soon sink in.

Finding your rib

The way you "love" and approach relationships dates all the way back to the very beginning of your existence.

From the moment, we are conceived in our mothers' wombs, we are being programmed. Programmed by words, affection, emotions, thoughts, and spirits; this programming or environment that we are immediately immersed into is known as a paradigm.

Paradigms simply put are other peoples' underlying, subconscious thoughts that directly affect a person's lifestyle and philosophies. We do not get to choose our parents or our paradigms, but we do get to choose if we will be similar or complete different products of those paradigms. The way people love is in direct correlation with the paradigms they have been exposed to. As for me, I grew up in an environment where love was propagated in the form of the man working, providing, enforcing his statutes upon the family. The women: my mama and my aunts, mostly stayed home and took care of the home.

My family is old-school. At some point in my life, I have personally witnessed all the men in my life solely providing for the family and truly finding enjoyment in it. Likewise, I have witnessed the women who stayed at home find their own share of enjoyment with being a wife and being readily available for their husbands and their children. Due to this type of exposure I have a desire to want to love my wife in the same manner.

All the women in my family (my aunts, not so much my cousins), are affectionate people. My mama and my aunt Kaye are certainly the most affectionate. They have always gone out of their way to express their love to me and they pretty much demanded it back from me. On the other hand, the men in my family, all except my uncle Ken and cousin Keith, are the exact opposite of affectionate. As a matter of fact, I have never heard any of them direct the word "love" to anyone other than the kids. My uncle Ken tells my aunt, Vanessa, he loves her. In fact, I have heard him say that on many occasions.

As for my household specifically, I have never in 26 years heard my pops tell my mama that he loves her. I am one-hundred percent sure that he does; he just does not express it verbally. It was only about six months ago that I ever saw him give her a kiss. It totally shocked me!

There have been times that I have seen my pops make other gestures that signified his approval of my mama, like smacking her on the butt in front of me. He didn't do it to be crude, but it was sort of a supplementation to the type of manhood he wanted for me. At least that's how I interpreted it. We are tough men, manly men, we love sports, talking trash, cussing, and constantly reiterating the fact that we oversee things. We didn't approve of men with earrings or pink shirts or any other thing that seemingly represented any level of femininity. We've become more flexible over the years. I have a pair of salmon colored shorts. When it came to the relationship counsel that I received from my pops, uncles, and cousins, it was simple and straightforward: **"you're the man! Don't ever get married until you are absolutely ready because there are too many women out here to think about settling down."**

I loved it when my uncles would say to me "what's up playa playa!" That made me feel like I was doing things right. Having only one woman was an absurdity to me. This was my paradigm, and what I would have to eventually conquer to find the love I wanted for my life.

Due to my uncertainty in choosing the right woman, I always brought my women home so that my mama and cousin Felicia could smoke them over and tell me whether I had a keeper. Over a course of five years, I took at least seven women to meet my family. Of the seven I brought home, there was only one that I truly wanted to be with. Ironically, she happened to be the very one that none of my family seemed to care for.

Everyone loved Riley. She was the picture-perfect woman for me in their eyes, and this really made me look deeper into our future together. I must admit,

Riley is an awesome woman. She is everything any sensible man could ever want or need, but I was rarely sensible when it came to relationships. No matter which woman I was involved with, minus one, I have always had this irrational fear that there was someone out there who was more suitable for me. I felt like there was something I was going to miss out on if I were to settle this early in the game.

One of the biggest mistakes I have ever made, and I still struggle with to this day is sharing too much information with my family about the problems that occur in my relationships. The fact that they love me warps their perspectives on the circumstances because they are naturally going to gravitate toward vindicating my actions. Not to mention when you expose problems to family, it makes it harder to accept that person back into your life. All your family will ever remember are the bad things you told them.

From the moment those bad thoughts are planted in their minds they become cynics. Earnestly believing that they had my best interest in mind, they adamantly objected when I attempted to express my love for certain women, quick to remind me of what they had done to hurt me. Knowing this would happen I would often shy away from speaking my true feelings about the one woman that I truly loved. There wasn't a chance of me ever expressing my feelings to the men in my family. I can hear them now:

"damn boy, you hen-pecked?"

"She got your nose so wide open; if she pissed in your face you would think it was raining!"

"Look at him; He got his little hearty broken!"

Then my pops would break out singing "I know you wanna leave me, but I refuse to let you go."

Followed by Uncle Ken's rendition of "Love TKO", then Uncle Barry would finish me off with "You too young to be damn Pussy-whipped! With his favorite line:

"Hell, if I was your age I wouldn't ever get married with all this trim out here."

Lastly, he'd give me his cure-all

"Go find you a BL*, a man needs him a good BL!"

You're probably wondering "how on earth can he be struggling with relationships with all the awesome advice and support he's receiving"

The only thing I hold on to though are the memories...the memories and moments trump all the negative feedback from aunts and cousins, all the trash talk from uncles and pops, and all the wildly subjective advice from friends, the memorable moments never leave me.

There is one woman above all the others; she stands head and shoulders above them all. When I think of her, the roaring storm in my heart is quieted. The winds stop hurling and the calm just rests on me. She is my muse. I love her without reason. Time has slipped in and put a slight wedge between us. I have grown more prideful and colder since her departure. She is the only women of whom I can genuinely say that I just want her to be as happy as she possibly can be, whether it's with me or some other man.

I have diligently tried for the last six years to mold one of my other women into her, but no matter how much time or effort they give me, it just does not compare. I find myself, year after year, trying to replace her, but it just does not seem to work. She is the purity of my soul, and all the contents therein. She is the ultimate compliment, and as my dog Dre so eloquently stated while walking with Sid in the park: "She's brown sugar."

Adam looked and exclaimed, "At Last! This is now, bone of my bone and flesh of my flesh! She will be called woman because she was taken from man."

I often wonder if Adam would have been so certain if he had seen or had sex with countless other women? Would he have been so sure of his proclamation? Then it occurred to me. After years of long-suffering, relationship woes, heartaches, uncertainty, insecurity, anguish, and just wanting to give up, that Adam could proclaim with such confidence because he prioritized.

Adam put his relationship with God and himself first. Secondly, he received his instruction from God. Thirdly, Adam worked. He worked! And then, God said, "it is not good that man is alone. I will make a helper-a compliment, who is just right for him." The reason I and most young men struggle **finding our rib** is because we want to try on every size, before being measured by God.

We consciously omit steps in the process, but we are so proud in our own understanding that we feel we can make our own rules and still be rewarded. This is one reason the institution of marriage suffers so drastically. Our minds have been perverted into believing that sex prior to marriage is simply sex. That sex is a harmless necessity. We don't use the word sin any longer. As long as people "love" that is all that matters. We're emotion-driven, and we ignore any advances of truth.

These things are a result of a perverted instruction which God plainly communicated to Adam and his woman in the Old Testament and is reiterated by Christ in the Gospels:

Matthew 19:4-5

> *"Have you not read the scriptures? They record that from the very beginning, God made them male and female. And he said, this explains why a man leaves his father and mother and is joined to his wife and the two are united as one."*

Identity, instruction, and obedience are the quintessential factors in my opinion. If you have an identity in God, then you can openly receive his instruction, which will certainly induce the submission of your own will to obediently follow the perfect will of God.

Be confident in who you know God has called you to be. Without confidence, the vision will inevitably be impaired. Without the vision, there can be no fulfillment. Without fulfillment, the relationship serves no purpose and is then downgraded to making money, having sex, or just raising some kids you had together. And these things are all certainly key elements, but the mission is to leave behind a legacy that your great grandsons will honor you for.

This all brings me to my final point. It all boils down to commitment. Once you have identity and fellowship with God through Christ and the Holy Spirit, once you have received your instruction, after you have diligently begun to work and remain obedient, the last thing for you to do is find someone that compliments you well and provokes you to be the very best you can be. When these channels have been established the rest falls on the shoulders of the man. It is a man's responsibility to commit and ensure the woman continually feels loved and secure.

What is Love?

Just the other night, I was talking with big Money and Stack. Money told me something that his pops had told him, **"When it comes to relationships, your woman doesn't have to love you. It's your job to love her."**

Not long after, while in church my spiritual father, Apostle Tommy Twitty said something very similar that provoked my manhood and understanding of love. He said, **"God never instructed the woman to love a man. A woman is supposed to respect and submit to her husband."**

He referenced:

Ephesians 5:25-28 (MSG)

"Husbands, go all out in your love for your wives, exactly as Christ did for the church—a love marked by giving, not getting. Christ's love makes the church whole. His words evoke her beauty. Everything he does and says is designed to bring the best out of her, dressing her in dazzling white silk, radiant with holiness. And that is how husbands ought to love their

wives. They're really doing themselves a favor—since they're already "one" in marriage."

These few verses articulated by the Apostle Paul here in Ephesians are the blueprint for any man that desires to have a wife with plans to grow and prosper in love and understanding with her.

This is an ultimate challenge because it puts men in a very vulnerable state. A state that is often forgone simply because no man wants to grant any person, not just a woman, this seemingly absurd degree of power over them. Yet, as we grow in understanding and we come to know love, we find that it is necessary.

Love is the absolutely irrational quest for fulfillment. It is complemented by faith, action, and persistence. Love by way of verbal communication can be pathetically articulated at best. No man can accurately define his love for his wife. He uses his foundational guidelines to ensure that his love is functional, but he can in no way describe his love to any person that would evoke in their heart what he knows to be real in his heart.

To begin the unfolding of such an impactful question we must understand that no two person's circumstances are the same. In knowing that one key piece of information, man can approach the question with diplomacy and attempt to provide the best-rounded answer that he, with his own limited perspective and level of understanding, can provide.

As for me, I believe that for anything to be absolutely defined that there must be a constant involved. In fact, it must be an eternal constant, one that transcends all known boundaries of time, and all finite knowledge of man. This eternal constant, God, is the ultimate measure of all things and without him nothing that is can be defined.

Now that the stage has been set, the question: **"What is Love?"** can begin to be answered... God is love. Therefore, love is all things. There is nothing in this world that is not a derivative of love. Even hatred and evil, though they seem to be the exact opposites of love, we know where they come from. If God created all creatures and granted freewill then the conception of evil is not a reflection of God, rather, it reflects the perversion of the creature's willingness to act out the perfect, ever-rewarding instruction of an infinitely wise God.

Love is quality. For that reason, it cannot be counted, but we can exhaust ourselves trying to put its value into perspective because we as humans have an insatiable desire for quantitative solutions. Love can only be measured by the extent or intrinsic value that one places on his own life because that is the asking price of love; your life. The value placed on your life is indicative of the value you place on love.

Love is expressed in different ways by different people, but one thing is explicitly constant in all ensuing love affairs: your foundational truths about life, existence, and humanity should always influence the way that you love yourself and especially another human being. These foundational truths serve as a template that will allow those you are in a relationship with to accurately judge the love you are giving them. Truth is the grading scale to prove if the love you speak of and the level of love you live out are consistent with one another.

The consistency that is established through this evaluation will directly impact the level of trust that is shared within the relationship. Trust is adhesive, which is applied through communication. Love is a zero-sum game. Therefore, God instructs us not to have any other gods before him. It is also why we should leave our fathers' and mothers to cleave to one husband or one wife. Anything that you give your attention to takes away from your ability to love whatever is on the other end of the spectrum.

If that thing has not specifically been identified as a supplemental agent, then it is a hindrance to your ability to fulfill your commitment to God or to your relationship. Many people say that the opposite emotion of love is indifference. I used to agree with the notion until I truly started to understand the absolute nature of love.

Indifference is not the opposite of love. Indifference has no true destructive power. It doesn't take an individual out of the presence of God or pervert the practical use of encoded DNA within our genome. Indifference has never lifted one to heights of greatness or provoked a person to do anything that would cause their story to be echoed in eternity. Indifference is not the opposite of love; it's exactly what it implies: meaninglessness.

The opposite of love is LUST. My pastor Tommy R. Twitty gave a brilliant definition of lust. He said,

"Lust is your desire for something or someone that is not intended for you."

Lust has the power to stain perfection causing blessed people to be exiled from the very presence of God.

Genesis 3: 6, 23-24

6 The woman could see that the tree was beautiful, and the fruit looked so good to eat. She also liked the idea that it would make her wise. So, she took some of the fruit from the tree and ate it. Her husband was there with her, so she gave him some of the fruit, and he ate it.

23 So the Lord God forced the man out of the Garden of Eden to work the ground he was made from.

24 God forced the man to leave the garden. Then he put Cherub angels and a sword of fire at the entrance to the garden to protect it. The sword flashed around and around, guarding the way to the tree of life.

A beautiful liar can make you believe that the truth isn't so beautiful. This is the conception of lust in the mind which is the very thing that caused the woman to "see that the tree was beautiful". When we stop seeing through our instruction, what we hold as truth will always be less attractive than the perverted lie.

Lust itself is not the destruction. It is the lustful nature that leads to destruction. Wherever lust is, love cannot abound and wherever love is lust cannot exist. Love is the true understanding of implications. Lust is the active denial of all things that lead to life. Love and lust are uncannily indistinguishable to those who have never been trained to pinpoint the ill-nature of lust. For this reason, many people: young and old make commitments and agree to terms that they have been tricked into believing were the best thing for their lives, but in all actuality, it was the beginning of the worst drought they will have ever experienced.

Lust will never induce fulfillment. It can't! The very essence of lust is to rob your purpose in life. The human condition truly gets the best of us at times. We as humans do not have the ability to control our natural desires if we have not the fortitude and transcended enlightenment of self that grants us unblemished perspective. Love is the absolute consideration of others, while lust only pushes personal agenda.

In the Bible, **1 John 2:16** we are warned: *"For the world offers only a craving for physical pleasure, a craving for everything we see, and pride in our achievements and possessions. These are not from the Father, but are from this world."*

In summary, the only thing the world has to offer us is lust. If the world offers lust that means, there can be no offering of love. The same writer earlier in the bible says in the gospel of **John 3:16** *"For God loved the world so much that he gave his one and only Son so that everyone who believes in him will not perish but have eternal life."*

As I mentioned earlier, love is the only giver of life. It was love that had to come, incarnate, to a world full of lust to give us all the brief opportunity to communicate our love to others as Christ so willingly communicated it to us through his selfless deeds.

This is my charge to you...if you believe that you truly want to accept the call to love: You must totally forsake all personal desires and become absolutely vulnerable because love has no contingencies. Love is a total commitment from the very moment you enter covenant until a qualifying event puts it asunder. If it's love you seek, you must be willing to completely lose yourself. You must die so that love can live, forgetting all the things of the past that sparked interest in your soul and focus only on the new things.

Love is a journey with winding roads. There are no exact answers to the questions love present. You just have to be willing to fight. Each day love will present a new challenge, but to the one who's willing to endure the hardships of love the reward is everlasting. Love is our greatest possible achievement. It is the one thing every man can do, it is the one thing that gives us all identity and purpose. Love alone is the only agent in the universe that can never fail.

If any man speaks of love in any regard, we should be able to justifiably presume that he has become a student of prioritization in this same faculty. No man can love without the conscious practice of prioritizing. When given a choice, a man that truly loves will always choose the option that solidifies his professed love for his respective love.

For we know through wisdom that what a man says has no true value, but through his actions, we can accurately calculate the true value of the man and subsequently place value on his word.

No man should be assumed a student of love if his works don't precede him. Love is not a matter of blind estimation, there is an extremely blunt template for love. Love needs not to be explained, except for the purpose of comforting the heart of those within your covenant.

Love is a belief system that creates actions. Those actions then become the reinforcement for beliefs. So, when a man loves, his imminent action should only make his love more resolute.

Love is a force that cannot be argued, it cannot be denied. Love is much like gravity, a constant energy that never changes, and impacts the entire universe. Unlike gravity though, love has no way of being tested without much sacrifice being made. To test the laws of gravity, a person could simply jump up in the air or step onto a scale. Love is much more complex and must be tested by fire.

I could truly go on forever about what love is, but I'll end with this last point that sums love up for me and hopefully it will have a similar effect on you.

God is love. This means that love, just like God is boundless and perfect. Love is not just a thing; it is the standard for all things. No one can truly know love without knowing God because they are one in the same. Love sent his son to die so that we (the world) could be saved through faith. Again, I say, love is our greatest possible achievement, it is our greatest hope, and with love anything is possible.

PRIDE GOES BEFORE A

FALL (A Love Chronicle reflection)

We told each other it was love, but we lacked love's capacity. There was a sublime lust that rested upon us. There was no tangible darkness, but the revelation was imminent.

She spoke with a convincing tone. Quite eerie, if the truth be told; one story after another she revealed. There was an unbridled desire for validation. She needed to be recognized. Reduced by the shadows of accomplishment, lost in the trenches of individuality, she needed a purpose. She spoke eloquently. It was a marvelous display of words and dramatization; perfect in fact. I was hooked. She was the perfect bait. I was the perfect catch. Her sweet words lulled my spirit to sleep. I wasn't confident then, I was cocky, and I loved it. People loved me for it and the ones that didn't could've gone to hell for all I cared. Life was not just a show, it was my show.

I was on top of the world. I was young, handsome, and intelligent, my friends were super cool, I was a super athlete and I was poised for the MLB draft in two to three short years. There wasn't anything in the world that couldn't have been apprehended under my own volition. Women just came with the territory. I was the man long before Aloe Blacc recorded his hit record!

My life was perfect, and a perfect man needed a perfect trophy piece. She was that perfect piece, validated by none other than herself.

Everything that went on, she was right there. It became second nature. She laughed at every joke; she internalized every word, not to grow but to capture the heart of the untamed beast. She wanted to be the one. This was her chance to establish her dominance amongst the group.

When a person is seeking to make a name for themselves, power is always the motivating factor. Power and lust go hand in hand. At the time, I was perceived as the alpha-male. I always made the grandest gestures, I spoke the loudest, and I dominated every scene that I could. My flamboyance made me an easy target. She was precise in her calculations, and subtlety was her strong tower.

She knew I had an insatiable ego. This known ego would be the key element in my destruction and the integral piece for her sustaining the majority stake in my ability to make rational choices.

One night we were in the room watching Dream Girls, our favorite movie, and the perpetual movie night selection. She had just got in from practice and showering. Prior that day she had already told me that her legs were sore, and she needed a massage. So, I, being the gentleman and friend that I had grown to be gladly obliged her; but we both knew the truth. That night was the initiation of the demise of my egotistical reign.

Soon after this night, the news spread like wildfire. The women that I was currently involved with all hated me because they felt betrayed by the fact that I would enter a relationship with this woman after I had adamantly and consistently expressed our platonic friendship. The day she told the twins changed everything! They were a part of our tight-knit circle of friends. I was sexually involved with one of them.

The news was shocking. More than anything, it was the undertone of manipulation and the diminishment of loyalty that caught everyone off guard. Ironically, those were the very factors that fueled our passion. This was an immediate, head over hills relationship that was riddled with lust and unwarranted pleasures. I believed in my heart that this was truly the fairy tale love that I longed for in my life.

Wisdom Moment: The enemy is crafty, but God is just. Let me explain: Love is something that I have coveted my entire life. I live for it. I have a tremendous love that is alive in me, but for my entire life, up until recently, I was always under the impression that love is just a sublime emotion that provokes choices. I am wiser now. Love is a choice that manages emotions. When you choose to love and understand the implications of that choice, you'll always act consistently with love regardless of what you feel.

At this point in my life, I was excited because this woman had an amazing body, she was smart, and she said all the right things. She was, in my mind exactly what I wanted my wife to be. This was long before I had any understanding of what ungodly soul ties were.

The craftiness of the enemy; lack of wisdom, discipline, and discernment on my behalf sent me into a whirlwind of instability, temperamental behavior, uncontrollable emotions, imminent retaliation (in some form), and suppression of truth. What was happening at this point in my life was a phase I like to call "CRASHING". I had been speeding down a dark alley and the road was finally winding down.

We were inseparable at this point. We spent every moment together. That spring break, we were together every moment of every single day and I don't think we wore clothes the entire time we were at the house. It was like a honeymoon, except for the one blaring fact!

One night while indulging in one of our episodic sexual rants, while crying, she said to me **"George, promise me you'll never leave me!"** I was ABSOLUTELY GONE!!! This was the night I committed it all. Every ounce of pride, every priority, every rational thought, she was in control of them all. She dominated me! That much power isn't very becoming of any person with tendencies such as hers.

My current state was totally foreign to me. I didn't know who I was; I couldn't feel unless she was there to induce it, I didn't think unless she was there giving clues. I was a programmed automaton, and she had the only security code. The only out I had was suicide. I never attempted it, but I often entertained the thought. I hated myself for allowing this to happen. Prior to this relationship, I dominated everything!

No matter how hard I tried, I couldn't snap out of it. I tried having sex with other women. I tried focusing on baseball, and I loved ball more than anything. I even began helping my friends with homework and studying. Nothing helped. The day was coming when she would eventually leave me. I was of no use to her anymore. I had become a puppet. Helplessly, I sat, watching my pride diminish with each waking day. She never intended to hurt me, but she certainly didn't have time to rebuild a broken boy who had lost all knowledge of what it meant to become a man.

Wisdom Moment: When we are young, we have not a heart for understanding; we only have hearts for passion. We desire to feel something new. Something that surpasses historical levels of euphoria, we have no regard for our humanity, and we pursue our flesh relentlessly. Propaganda tells us that living wildly in our youth will be our greatest achievement; because when we're "old" the younger days will be the only thing that gives us joy. The reminiscence of those fiery, passion-filled nights will be the testimonies for the history books that we lived, that we partied, that we conquered every known aspect of morality and intrinsic value. We became gods… "Yeah, we were gods."

She was on her way out; I was all the way in. She tried on several occasions to make it seem as if it were her love for Christ that propelled her to want to pull away from this trying relationship, but I knew the truth. I was like the new video game that gets thrown to the side once all the levels have been conquered.

At this stage in my life, I had nothing else to offer her. She saw the massive potential, but potential, in all actuality is equivalent to zero. There was this other guy that had caught her eye. It's embarrassing to admit after all these years, but my freedom has come. I'm no longer hiding.

He was a handsome cat no doubt about that. Seemed cool, smooth dude, dressed well, spoke well. I understand the attraction now. There was only one problem with it all. She was supposed to love me! She wasn't supposed to see this guy. As I stated, I was only potential. I had no money, no car, and no apartment. Nothing… *(and I know you're thinking,* **"you were a college student!"** *True. But I felt like I needed more)*

For the first time in my life, I felt true jealousy creeping into my psyche. It was taking over; like a terminal infectious disease. I was paranoid. Suddenly, my clothes didn't fit right on my body, my dick felt small, my words carried no weight, I didn't feel smart, and on top of it all, I felt like everyone could see it.

Depression was something that I had been exposed to first hand as a child, so I knew that's exactly where I was heading. The only things I knew how to do well were being cocky and telling lies. So, in a desperate attempt to stave off the inevitable, I began to indulge with as many women as I could. I filled their head with all types of commitment rubbish.

There wasn't anything I wouldn't do or any barrier that I wouldn't cross to assure myself that I had gotten over this hurt. Every time I seemed to get to a place where I could relax, she always came back, crushing me again. I could not say no to her. Anything she wanted, anytime she wanted it I did it. One night around 4 a.m. she called. I was lying in Pride hall in bed with an esteem booster.

Me: "Hello?"

Her: "Heeyyy George!"

Me: "What's up? You good?"

Her: "Yeah, but I'm really tired! I just want to go to sleep but I have this paper to type before class in the morning."

Me: "Where are you?"

Her: "Near campus..."

Me: "Well come over here, you can use my laptop."

Her: "Really? Ok. Be there shortly."

It's 4 a.m.!!! I just left a young lady in the middle of the night, disturbing her sleep, then sprinted across campus to get back to my room to allow the woman that has crushed me use my laptop for the paper *she* needs to type for *her* class! She came in with her bags; I could tell she was exhausted. She sat on the couch and attempted to type her paper. She was sleep before she completed the first paragraph.

Then the light bulb went off! This was my chance to prove to her again that I loved her and that she should be with me. When she woke up that next morning, there it was! Her assignment; fully formatted and typed just the way her professor instructed *(I also had to change the settings on the computer to be sure it didn't hibernate before she woke up to see the completed work).*

Looking back, there is no way she could have known I was going to type that paper for her. I honestly don't think she even considered it, and that is more reason why I was certain this was going to work! But it didn't change one thing.

Wisdom Moment: If a person doesn't want to be with you, there is nothing you can do to convince them that they should be. Spare yourself the shame and save yourself the time.

One day, while chilling all alone in my room I began to pray. I didn't pray for forgiveness, I didn't pray for God's perfect will, I didn't pray that my swing got better or that my family remained safe. I prayed and asked God for another opportunity to experience feelings this strongly for a woman. I prayed for a gentle woman who was a friend, one that was athletic, pretty, smart, and God-fearing, a woman that would love me unconditionally. This was my prayer. God answered it. But I made the same mistakes...

Wisdom Moment: Never pray that God sends you anything. Pray that God prepares you for His divine will. Giving a car to a 10-year old and telling him to drive safely is foolish, but we never stop to think of ourselves as that 10-year old under the wheel and out of His will. God will sometimes grant wishes so that we can see that we aren't ready. His permissive will is different from his perfect will. The things God allows us to do often teach us the hard lessons that we would not have to learn if we would just exercise faith while practicing patience and humility.

It is never God's intention for us to suffer, but our own desires lead us into temptation causing us to pervert the perfected plan God has for our lives. This perfect plan would provide for us and make us prosperous in every aspect of life, and ultimately serves all of humanity.

Do not make wishes. Make preparations.

DAYS THAT TURN OUR LIVES AROUND

One day in the spring of 2012, my final semester at A&T, as I was walking through the cafe, headphones in, music polluting my soul, my man Nelson stopped me and asked me, **"Aye G, who are you living for today? God or the Devil?"** He planted a seed of critical, inescapable thought in my heart that was far gone from me. The thought led to conviction. Truth was, I had no reverence for God, I was indifferent.

Heaven, at this phase in my life, seemed too good for a sinner like me. The eternal fire of hell seemed more practical for an ice-cold soul like my own. Somehow, his question ignited something inside me. It evoked my conscience; which had been long forgotten and discarded as weak emotion. My soul was stirred up this day.

All the pain and anguish I had caused in my past suddenly began to weigh on me. Sex was beginning to convict my spirit. Lying no longer seemed like the right thing to do. I had previously stopped gambling after a night in Texas with the boys where I lost over $300 cash on the tunk table. The most shocking thing of all was that I no longer had the desire to be **The Man**. I wanted to be **A Man**.

I latched on to the only thing that I figured could save my soul from this ruin; **the truth**. Truth that my pops had instilled deep inside me long ago. I began to dig my way out of this misery that I walloped in for nearly six years all because I was not willing to deal with my arrogance and prideful ways.

Wisdom Moment: God works in eternity. Therefore, the truth is an eternal entity. A man can only shun truth for so long before he must meet his maker and take account for all he has done. Our days upon this earth are numbered. The sooner we come to grips with the truth, the sooner we can begin to live our lives.

God will get your attention! Let me say that again, GOD WILL GET YOUR ATTENTION!!! And he will utilize anything under the sun to do so. He is the master of the universe. Unfortunately for me, it took losing Riley, my best friend because I was too prideful to express my grief and admit that I too, can be hurt.

As I mentioned in the beginning, God allows us to do things, and though he sees us through, we must accept the consequences of our choices. Now that I have grown to be a little wiser, I see now why God wants us to avoid certain things. He loves us; therefore, he instructs us. When we don't heed the instructions, the things we desire most in life become the hardest to attain.

Again, I say: Truth is eternal. If you'll accept it, freedom and joy will be yours all the days of your life.

My prayer is that you take from my Chronicles some essentials that can be used in your life. My pride and my own perverted vision of what my life was "supposed to be" caused me to thwart every blessing God wanted to send. The one blessing that I thought was God-sent turned out to be a miscarried hope of my perversion. In other words, God saved me from what I thought I needed.

Creative Imagination

In the world-renowned book *Think and Grow Rich*, Chapter 11: Sex Transmutation, it pinpoints 10 mind stimuli. The first and most powerful stimulus is **"The desire for sex expression"**. Before expounding on the point, I believe it is necessary to state that Napoleon Hill's book *Think and Grow Rich* is one of the best sellers of all times and revered to many as the number one book to aid in one's creation of great wealth and prosperity.

The desire for sex expression induces what Napoleon Hill calls "creative imagination" which is also likened to being genius. When sexual desire consumes the mind of a person they assume a power of genius proportions to accomplish things that they, under normal circumstances could not conjure up the ability to attain. Sex is powerful. As I mentioned: It is number one on the list of Napoleon Hill's mental stimuli. As I gaze at the world we live in; I see why sex drives nearly every market. Sex is profitable. Although, it can certainly be destructive in nature when one lacks understanding or lives devoid of the necessary outlets to positively channel this sex energy.

Now, I am going to attempt to tie this together in a way that will no longer allow us to write this topic off as mere coincidence. As we peer into the music industry; look closely at the explicit sexual content with lyrics and videos. Godlessness is undoubtedly the agenda being pushed onto culture, especially onto the younger generations. And sexuality is an integral player. Which to me is revealing because behind every propagandized youngster there is an implication of an irresponsible adult. Rap music, though I love some of the songs, is misogynistic. In their defense, I do not necessarily believe this is the exclusive intent of all rappers, but it is certainly debatable. What I do feel though, is that money eradicates all fetters of morality. That's not all. The fervent pursuit and subsequent acquisition of money seemingly vindicates men and women from nearly all moral responsibilities. When you are rich far beyond necessity and free from the burden of accountability the combination can become deadly. The music that is produced now and socially accepted solidifies this very sentiment.

These "artists" are promoted by the industry to pervert the minds of audiences to fill their wallets. I do not blame them for being businessmen, but it would be awesome if they could dispel some of the lyrics as pure entertainment and not matter of fact. Unless of course, all the lyrics were entirely true. Personally, I find it quite impossible for all the things being spoken in the lyrical content to be true because these individuals are consummate professionals and masters of their craft.

The crafting of these lyrics plants a desire for sex expression within the minds of the generations. These seeds grow and become actions. Repetitive actions become a lifestyle, and a life of repetitiveness is nearly impossible to reverse. So, I ask: *Is it a coincidence that the music and entertainment industries are the paramount conduits for this brand of illicit sensuality that undermines humanity?*

Looking at the character of Satan as described in the Bible, we can arrive at the sensible conclusion that it is bigger than just music and entertainment. In the book of John chapter 14 verse, 30 here is what Jesus speaks **"I will not talk with you much longer. The ruler of this world is coming. He has no power over me."**

Here Jesus describes Satan as the ruler of this world. Many would ask **"How is Satan the ruler of this world if God created it?"** The answer is simple. God did create the world but in the beginning of mankind in the Garden of Eden, when man ate the fruit that God instructed him not to eat, the world (mankind) was then transmuted from perfection to imperfection. Man gave his keys to the enemy. The only way to get those keys back is through Christ.

For this reason, **2 Corinthians 5:17 (NKJV)**

"Therefore, if anyone is in Christ, he is a new creation; old things have passed away; behold, all things have become new."

Our acceptance of Jesus Christ as our personal savior no longer makes us a part of this world. Our sins are washed away by his blood, our perspectives become totally new, which ultimately compels us to live lives that others would look at and desire to emulate, inducing but not limited to soul salvation.

Another verse that accredited much power and influence on Satan is **Ephesians 2:2** *"in which you once walked according to the course of this world, according to the prince of the power of the air, the spirit who now works in the sons of disobedience"*

This basically means that Satan is so busy that the very air is contaminated with sin. And ironically when anything is being broadcasted to the masses the very phrase used is *"on the air"* which means that images and sounds are currently being transmitted or broadcasted via television, radio, or internet.

Many people, including me at one point, attempt to write all of this off as mere coincidence and make claims that there is no God, implicitly making the story of Satan false as well. But the claims do not disprove what the inspired word of God says, nor have these claims ever been able to totally eradicate faith from the hearts of a majority of spiritually enlightened beings upon this planet.

Aforementioned are some of the functionalities of Satan but what I am going to do now is describe his personal attributes as they were given in the Bible.

Isaiah 14:11-17

11 Your pride has been sent down to Sheol.

The music from your harps announces the coming of your proud spirit.

Maggots will be the bed you lie on,

and other worms will cover your body like a blanket.

12 You were like the morning star,

but you have fallen from the sky.

In the past, all the nations on earth bowed down before you,

but now you have been cut down.

13 You always told yourself,

"I will go to the skies above.

I will put my throne above God's stars.

I will sit on Zaphon, the holy mountain where the gods meet.

14 I will go up to the altar above the tops of the clouds.

I will be like God Most High."

15 But that did not happen.

You were brought down to the deep pit—Sheol, the place of death.

16 People will come to look at your dead body.

They will think about you and say,

"Is this the same man

who caused great fear in all the kingdoms on earth,

17 who destroyed cities

   and turned the land into a desert,

who captured people in war

   and would not let them go home?"

Ezekiel 28:12-19

12 "Son of man, sing this sad song about the king of Tyre. Say to him, 'This is what the Lord God says:

"'You were the perfect man—

   so full of wisdom and perfectly handsome.

13 You were in Eden, the garden of God.

You had every precious stone—

   rubies, topaz, and diamonds,

   beryls, onyx, and jasper,

   sapphires, turquoise, and emeralds.

And each of these stones was set in gold.

   You were given this beauty on the day you were created.

   God made you strong.

14 You were one of the chosen Cherubs

   who spread your wings over my throne.

I put you on the holy mountain of God.

You walked among the jewels that sparkled like fire.

15 You were good and honest when I created you,

but then you became evil.

16 Your business brought you many riches.

But they also put cruelty inside you, and you sinned.

So I treated you like something unclean

and threw you off the mountain of God.

You were one of the chosen Cherubs

who spread your wings over my throne.

But I forced you to leave the jewels

that sparkled like fire.

17 Your beauty made you proud.

Your glory ruined your wisdom.

So I threw you down to the ground,

and now other kings stare at you.

18 You did many wrong things.

You were a very crooked merchant.

In this way, you made the holy places unclean.

So I brought fire from inside you.

It burned you!

You burned to ashes on the ground.

Now everyone can see your shame.

19 "'All the people in other nations

were shocked about what happened to you.

What happened to you will make people very afraid.

You are finished!'"

Both Old Testament prophets are describing the beauty, splendor, and gifts of Lucifer, The morning star. They are both depicting the beauty and power that God granted to Lucifer and explaining how that beauty eventually corrupted the mind of Satan which ultimately led to him being cast down and becoming the ruler of this world. With this depiction of Satan now in our minds, let's refocus on this desire for sex expression and think candidly about the types of music and television shows that we truly enjoy watching. Is there not an uncanny connection in this?

Satan's intent is to totally pervert the word of God. We have engrafted to the idea that any pleasures are good for us. Relegating the Devil's function in the world only to pain or obvious evils, but I'm here to serve notice that he's much craftier than we have given him credit for being.

We will never be tempted by things we do not desire. My challenge to you is to look at your life. Ask yourself what is it that you truly desire? Then ask yourself: have your desires caused you to become sinful in your thoughts and actions? If you are not able to rightfully divide the word of truth, you have been deceived. Satan has, in fact, made his move and perverted your thinking.

Be mindful that exhaustion from pleasure is more demoralizing to a nation than the struggles with pain. We must be certain that our acts are aligned with truth and not driven by our animal nature. It all goes back to our understanding of love and our willingness to accept the truth. Satan is the father of lies. If any lie becomes a conceived practicality in our lives, then the love of the Father is not within us. This is what the Apostle Paul speaks in **Romans 12:2**

Don't change yourselves to be like the people of this world, but let God change you inside with a new way of thinking. Then you will be able to understand and accept what God wants for you. You will be able to know what is good and pleasing to him and what is perfect.

Our thinking is the only thing that will bring forth convictions. Conviction induces truth. The truth shall set us free indeed. Making us new creatures in Christ and alienating us from the world that is ruled by the prince of the air. The purpose of all of this is to pinpoint the fact that our sexual natures are given to us by God. God knows what he's doing. Consumption awareness is a major key. Whatever a man consumes is inevitably what he will become. You cannot eat perverted truth and expect to produce a pure, fulfilled life.

My Fragmented soul

The reason for descriptively depicting the relationships of my past was not to embarrass or expose any young woman. The purpose was to paint a picture of the truth that isn't uncharacteristic in this generation. In fact, for many young men, it is a badge of honor.

I am here to dispel the myth amongst men that unbridled sexuality is an achievement that induces self-confidence, esteem, or manhood. Unwarranted pleasure will always be accompanied by ruin. It destroys the soul. I was under the impression that I could literally bang my way back to monogamy. This philosophy begat many passionate nights with young women I had fantasized about.

My good friend and spiritual brother Wild B once said to me: **"If you can't be pleased by one woman, a million women won't even come close to satisfying you."** This was a remarkable comment. He was right! With every new woman I laid down with all I could imagine was a newer one.

My mind was intrigued by the thought of new coochie. I abhorred my conscience. In efforts to remain in sexual bondage, I turned my heart's thermometer down as low as it would go. I rehearsed my words. I prepared my speeches and planned my approaches. Women were easy; too easy in fact. Common sense told me that anything this easy was dangerous for me, but I had no control over myself. Sex and masturbation had become normative practice in my quest to prove to that I was the man and could make any woman feel the love she imagined was possible.

At one point, I earnestly believed that God disregarded my sin because I was "helping" young women see themselves as beautiful for the first time. Heck, I had even turned a young lesbian back straight.I was proud of myself for that. My high-mindedness had consumed me. The only thing that could have slowed me down at this point was "a unicorn" *(a woman who had it all)*.

The word of God tells us that pride always comes before a fall. Well, pride had certainly crept in once I hit the year mark of my newly found life of abstinence. I was beginning to feel that it was me that brought forth this new change and that I was self-efficient. This didn't last long.

My pride aroused my ensuing lust for something that the hand of God had protected me from for more than three hundred and sixty-five days. Temptation!!! The only difference from then up to this point was my total dependence on God to deliver me from the temptations. Now, I was depending on my own ability. In my mind, I truly believed that I was strong enough to pull away from any situation that would jeopardize me slipping back into that pit of disaster again, but I was only lying to myself.

After only a few nights hanging with a young lady, I ended up right between her legs. Here's the thing with backsliding. You don't feel yourself slipping until you have crossed the line. Then there is an enormous amount of guilt that accompanies the action. What we discount the most, is the new war that has just been declared on our minds, hearts, and soul. I was hooked again. And it didn't take long at all.

We ignorantly, in my case foolishly underestimate the power of nature. If a man and a woman spend time together regularly, sexuality is going to emerge in one form or another. Over the last few years I have learned much about myself and how insecure I have been during different segments of my life. Not insecure about myself per se, more so in the opinions of those who love me. I have always wanted my family to view me as respectful and teachable.

In many instances, it has held me back. There are many things that I don't say to refrain from being offensive. I often shun truth to keep the peace but that leaves me with unrest in my soul. This unwillingness to be truthful has also spilled over into all my other relationships. The poet wrote, **"there is nothing enlightened about shrinking so that others don't feel insecure around you."**

Even fearless men have fears. My fear of not being received by people cripples my effectiveness in life. Coincidentally, it's my unique perspective that gives me my passion for helping people. This fear has stifled my relationships because I tell myself that what I desire doesn't exist. It tells me that I am too picky or that I'm being ridiculous because no woman is perfect. I'm not looking for perfection though...I'm just looking for the woman that is right for me. It has taken me all this time to finally realize that I have never holistically loved any woman who came into my life. First, I had to get an understanding of the absoluteness of love that only exists in God.

Although, I can say that there is one woman who captured my affection like no other young lady ever has. There have been instances where it felt uncannily like what I know love to be now. As well as some strongholds formed from those relationships that still plague my imagination to this day. But I have never felt genuinely confident that my quest for love was over. I have never given my all in a relationship and honestly, the mere thought alone scares me. It scares me because I have had countless women that have told me that I was the **"man for them"**. Hearing that often triggered this thought in my mind: **"I wonder what they'd feel/say if I was sincerely committed?"**

Hearing women make this statement assured me that people fall in love with potential. They project a path for you in their minds and if you don't follow their trajectory they will eventually abandon ship. So here I am...a student of love. In some cases, a professor of love for those that may reach out to me for instructions on how to procure or secure a love. Ironically, I can give all the necessary advice for others but there seems to be nothing that I have that works for me. For a while, I thought this made me a hypocrite, but I see clearer now. This advice only works for the individual that has fully committed him or herself to the relationship. Something I have yet to do in my life.

What I have managed to do though is create some very strong soul ties that were terribly difficult to shake. I thank God, I took to writing; it has really helped me express myself to myself in a way that I could never do to a woman. I'm here. A twenty-six-year-old God-fearing young man that loves love. Every fiber of my being desires to love a woman. I have studied love. I have learned its ways. I have taken tests and failed miserably on many occasions and I'm certain I'll never get anything absolutely right, but my intent is to get it right.

Lord my current request is that you rid my heart of all the confusion. Free me from the guilt of my past. Silence the cries of the sons and daughters that I foolishly executed. Hug my special son. Tell him his daddy is sorry and that your love far exceeds any love that I could have ever attempted to give him here. Father, soothe my heart from the pain. I want to end it once and for all. Restore my love. Restore my trust, and as you redeem me and my bad debts, I promise to stay in your will, I don't want you to ever forsake me. I am useless alone. I am nothing apart from you. Don't ever allow me to leave your side. Spell out danger for me plainly so that I can shun my stubbornness and pride to clearly see your plan for my life. This is my entire truth Father. This is my purge from sorrow and regret.

Stick your mighty hand back into the dust and reform me. Make me a man. I want to be righteous. I desire to be whole. Make me humble. Give me wisdom. Grant me understanding. Make me a leader. I want to be prosperous in my soul and in business. Give my mind's eye affluent vision. Give my heart discernment. Order my steps, Father. When I fall never let go of my hand. Correct me. Cover me. Give me children that I can raise up to be seekers and servants of your kingdom. Finally, and most importantly; I just want to thank you for saving me. I will never forget where you brought me from. Use me as your mighty instrument. Let my testimony be sweet music the ears of the generations. God, I am yours and you are mine. Amen.

IRRESPONSIBLE MALES

One of the saddest things I have witnessed is young women who suffer at the hands of irresponsible males. I use the word male intentionally. Boy is probably the best word. Man is undeserving. But male is sufficient.

When it comes to sexuality, men are far less likely to be upfront about the reality we're dealing with pertaining to our sex lives: *(i.e. sex partners, STDs, soul ties, and brokenness.)* As a result, we have taken away the woman's power to choose. No person can make an educated decision if they don't have all the facts. Everything is marginalized to emotion. Emotionalized realities are killing us. We have taken the truth out of living and made life a fantasy.

I recall many instances in which I was suspicious that I could possibly have an STD. Did I go get checked out by a clinic or Doctor? Sure. But only after I had unprotected sex with a young woman first to see if she would alert me. And if she didn't report back to me that something was wrong, I assumed everything was good. That was irresponsible on my part. And I was no exception. This is the case for many young men and women alike. Sexual irresponsibility is causing women and men all over the world to be broken and convinced that there is no hope for sustainable happiness in their futures.

I wish someone would have taught me. I wish I would have known that I was only harming myself. I wish I had known that I could never find what I was looking for this way. But I didn't... It has taken years of cycles for me to finally see that I was unfit for relationships. Thank God. Better late than never.

THE LONELIEST JOURNEY

The road to finding the love we deserve is the loneliest journey one will ever embark upon. It requires a stark sense of self, an unwavering faith, and an unblemished knowledge of purpose.

This is the road less traveled.

Our entire lives we have been conditioned by society and pop culture to feed our desires. They have shown us the joys of the moment, but they purposely omit the side effects of impulsive unwarranted behavior. The very essence of love requires one to know himself from the origination of thought to the implementation of its benevolence. We were designed by greatness to be nothing less than great.

Love is our highest level of communication. Without love, nothing that exists has any value. Love is a concerted truth that cannot be fortified by anything other than consummate action. The perils of love, one will never fully understand until they have fully committed to the journey.

Commitment: as defined by Merriam-Webster is

- *a promise to do or give something.*
- *A promise to be loyal to someone or something.*
- *The attitude of someone who works very hard to do or support something*

There are many factors that significantly lower one's propensity to commit, but the factors that have been the most prominent in my observations are fear of missing out, age, distrust, and casual sex.

The fear of missing out has single-handedly obliterated nearly every relationship I have ever attempted to have. It is an ongoing struggle. What the fear of missing out does to a person is poses this consuming idea of *"what if..."* in a person's mind. *What if* there is someone better? *What if* I don't love them like they love me? *What if* the sex isn't good? *What if* I really start to love them and my old girl comes back? So many questions arise, ultimately becoming insurmountable obstacles that often lead you to heartbreak or a long road to resentment. The age factor is something that has become more and more of an obstacle as time progresses. It will continually be a leading factor in why people do not commit in relationships. People honestly believe that there is a certain age in which love is something that should be sought after. Many people pretend to have a highly sophisticated plan that will surely induce true love once we have established lucrative careers, moved beyond the "wild years", and settled down.

I believe these sentiments are all true in part, but the one thing most people have not considered is all the inter-mingling with others they will be engaged in throughout this period of their lives. If this plan were perfectly executable for a vast portion of the individuals that attempt to utilize it, I believe that true unconditional love would be more affluent within the world today. There has been so little responsibility expressed and placed upon the younger generations that love may eventually become just a myth. It will become a quaint fairytale that many dream of procuring but have no inclination of how to manifest it within their lives.

Distrust is another factor that is rapidly disseminating throughout the culture. We have all been in situations in life that have left us doubting a person's motives. We have all been hurt by people. We have all been disappointed by people. And if we don't understand that people will always disappoint us in some way at some point, we have set impossible expectations and ultimately guaranteed failure.

There is a spirit or mindset of "unforgiveness" that plagues our generation. Not being able to forgive utterly decimates a person's ability to love. Forgiveness is the gift that keeps on giving. It is a key component for love to be conceived in the hearts and minds of all men and women. Trust is earned. With the focus on building trust in every person's mind, we set standards. Distrust forms when standards are initially met but subsequently breached by an unwarranted act or unaffectionate rant. This causes a person to be withdrawn from a situation to protect themselves from any ensuing pain because they have witnessed these signs before.

Distrust could even originate from the developmental stages of childhood. In my opinion, this form of distrust is the hardest to overcome. Individuals subjected to these types of environments form pathologies that are hardly amendable in short periods of time. They are victims of a paradigm that they have little understanding of and no dominion over. Being completed subjective in such an environment creates a disease within the individual that they must be able to recognize and admit to having. Without their confession, it will be virtually impossible to help rid them of this terminal relationship illness.

Another factor and the most widespread is casual sex. Casual sex strongly reinforces all the factors mentioned. It certainly caters to the "what if..." mindset that torments the those who fear missing out on something better. Casual sex certainly adds many implications to the age factor and prolongs the willingness of any seemingly young person to commit to a monogamous relationship *(we won't even mention abstinence)*.

Lastly, casual sex absolutely fortifies the distrust factor. We begin to think that all men or all women think exactly like the person we dealt with in our past relationships. These factors combine to create a fearful micro manager of emotion who eagerly advocates stoic behavior; a person who is often horny and readily willing to settle for anyone who subtly or explicitly expresses the same bestial sentiment. These factors create individuals who enter relationships without clearly defining relational roles or expectation *(aka "situationships")*. Situationships tarnish all chances of placing accountability on self or the significant other.

So, what has been created here is a false sense of self-preservation in which we believe in our hearts that we are just in these meaningless relationships to accommodate our personal needs, which are subject to change on any given day. All of this creates baggage. It adds wear and tear to our bodies, our spirits and ultimately our souls. These half-assed relationships corrode the foundation of a divine command given by God in the beginning: ***"Be fruitful and multiply."*** The journey of true love does not begin until you have explicitly defined yourself to yourself. You must internalize this definition and make it practical.

Once you have done this you must begin to set up boundaries that are conducive to the practical application of what you have defined. Your family, friends, and anyone else who could possibly be a hindrance to your new standard must be removed from the equation. Or they must be kept at a distance that does not deter fulfillment of the agreement you have made with yourself.

One major key to your success in this regard is not being afraid to feel what you feel. In other words, do not attempt to explain yourself to every person. You don't owe anybody, and the ones who deserve an explanation will not even require one.

My cousin Felicia always tells me, **"People expect others to be common."** I wholeheartedly agree. When people have placed such a lowly standard on you it's not because they do not truly believe in you. It stems from something much deeper; something that they have not come to terms with yet themselves: *they are common!* Naturally, they'll place an expectation on you that does not exceed their own and if by chance it does, it will not be to an accurate degree.

I reiterate: do your best to avoid explaining yourself to people who have that mindset. All your efforts to make them see your vision will be futile and ultimately dilute your concentration. Once you have internalized your definition, you have taken a new form. You are a new person. You cannot bring old habits into new pathologies. Those old habits will eventually morph you right back into the person you vowed never to be again.

Only the bravest of men find and keep their true soul mate because the task is daunting. True love calls for absolute vulnerability. The moment you decide to love a person you give them a key to your soul. They have the power to build you or ruin you. For this to happen, one must be totally secure within themselves. There cannot be any pressing insecurities or else the relationship will eventually be corrupted by jealousy, strife, or anger which all derive from fear.

In the book of Ephesians, chapter five verse twenty-five we find this charge to all men: *"Husbands, you must love your wives so deeply, purely, and sacrificially that we can understand it only when we compare it to the love the Anointed One has for His bride, the church."* This brand of love is rarely witnessed. In fact, I am not 100% sure that many in my generation have ever actually witnessed it firsthand.

Christ loved the church His "bride" so much that he gave his own life so that she could be justified through him. As men and husbands, this is our just duty. There is only one way that this love is viable; through Christ. If we do not follow in the footsteps and heed the instructions of Christ, we lack the wisdom or virtue to provoke this supreme feeling of compassion and selfless sacrifice.

Without Christ, the incarnate word of the Most-High God, love is a foreign concept to us all. For this reason, true love is the loneliest journey any man will ever embark upon because Christ calls men to a higher standard. Christ's standard is one that is attainable for all men who are willing, but there are only a chosen few who will ever experience this divine level of fulfillment and joy. The time is now. The question is: are you a man or woman who is willing to go the distance for the love you deserve?

Cheating the Process

My entire life I have always searched for a shortcut to greatness. I recently found out there isn't one; on any level! All the years I have spent searching have just been years of lollygagging around the same rudimentary challenges that could have easily conquered had I just been willing to put in the necessary work.

Just a relatively short time ago, I realized that my desire to cut corners--in school, sports and occupation have been replicated in all my relationships as well. I consider myself to be a pretty intelligent guy, but intelligence gets boring. Pushing the envelope was more daring. My intelligence gave me the edge I needed to manipulate systems to produce the thrill needed to remain interested.

Throughout my entire life, finding a way to deviate has been more challenging than status quo. It had nothing to do with malicious intent, there has always been a genuine disinterest in doing it the way everyone else did it. I never gave 100% yet I was still gifted enough to compete with the best.

Competing was not living up to my potential, but it kept me crawling forward. It seemed that I had something that others admired and some coveted. I did not have to study, work as hard in the weight room, or practice as hard, but on game days or test days finishing amongst the leaders was something I expected to do.

Here is my definition of cheating--**any activity a person consciously engages but doesn't give their best effort.** Cheaters are mediocre at best. Their lives, their love, their character, etc. Mediocre.

This worked for me my entire life. It was all that I had known. I didn't do it to be dishonest; I did it because it was invigorating and easy for me. At the time it seemed more rewarding. Unfortunately, I was too immature to see that serving my ego was suffocating my soul. This was a costly habit and eventually, I became dependent upon it.

I have reached a crossroads in my life now, as we all will, and I am faced with one of two choices:

1. Settle for a life that I know is not worthy of me
2. Man up and do what is necessary to complete the assignment that I know God has anointed me for.

The Resurgence of Impatience

Here I lay, March 22, 2014, more than a year since I have had sex or masturbated. It's 3:31 am... right here beside her, naked and very ashamed, holding her hand attempting to signify that everything is ok.

Lying to myself while attempting to soothing my own guilt with God's grace. I am the hypocrite. Can my soul be redeemed from the fiery torment that is so deserving of me? *(Once we have been deceived by illicit desires, we're immediately imprisoned by guilt. That is how the enemy works. He burns both ends of the candle.)*

"I want to serve God. I want to love God" ... is what I hear echoing in my heart but it's a lie. There is no practical truth in me. Actions justify words. My actions have proven yet again that I'm not fully submissive to the process. My heart is riddled with perversion and my desire for love is transmuted to lust yet again.

In my possession, I hold the keys to a young woman's soul. I am full of idolatry and I hate correction. The wisdom of life is in me, but close by is the lust of flesh, and pride of life. I am a sinner. I knew coming here wasn't a good idea, but I'm blinded by my own pride. I have removed God and replaced his sovereignty with my own agenda. Young women, please... Hear me crying from the depths of shame, young men take heed...no matter what you think; perversion is the destruction of love.

To penetrate the soul of a woman you haven't committed to is the ultimate treason. I cry aloud to all that will hear...forsake your own knowledge and find refuge in the presence of most high God. He is our only fortress. Again, Father, I have failed you... I hear you walking through the garden. I wish I had the courage to come out and face you but I'm too ashamed. I won't point a finger, but I understand why Adam did. When you know better, the guilt is too heavy a burden. My prayer Lord if I may? Please don't banish this young woman from the grounds. Send me. It is I that chose disobedience. She tried to stop me, but I was persistent. I became that Serpent of old.

Father, can I be forgiven again? Can you still use me in your kingdom? You have blessed me with understanding, but I ruin it with my doubts. If you turn away from me, where else can I go? You are the only help I know. I am a wicked man. My flesh seems to be ever-present. Why do I continue to do wrong when I know what you expect from me? God, are you listening? God...? Father, please...?

God *(in my thoughts)*: Why do you call me father? If you were my son would you not obey my commands? You speak of love and you have increased in knowledge, but you are cast away. Was it not I who granted you your eyes to see and your ears to hear? Why have you abandoned my instructions? Just like your fathers before you, you have chosen your own path and it certainly leads to destruction. Why do you relish treachery? Your love for iniquity leads you to slaughter. You are not my son, for I know my children when I call they hear my voice. Depart from me you son of rebellion, because of your wickedness I have forgotten your name!

This echoed in my heart, like the lines from a movie that had been memorized. I could literally feel judgment being passed on my soul. There was nowhere to turn, no one to call on, nowhere to hide. All I could do was lie there. Even in the midst of my shame, I could hear the gentle voice of my father still trying to correct me and save me, but guilt had set in.

There I was praying for forgiveness of one sin while I should have been focusing on what was about to happen next. You see, God is not surprised by our flesh. All of that praying and begging was just an episodic guilt trip. If I had been sincere about not wanting to abuse this young woman's body and wanting to stay in the will of God I would have gotten out of that bed and went home. Instead, I laid there drowning in my own sorrow while God was trying to save me from another snare. As soon as the refractory period had subsided, so had my acknowledgment of God. I was right back inside of her again! No less than fifteen minutes had passed.

Hear this: We will never sanctify our flesh! It will never happen; stop praying about it! What we can do though is bring our flesh into submission by not putting ourselves in positions where we are tempted by lustful desires. God will always provide a way of escape from sin. God is proactive. We are mostly reactive. And when it is time to think forward, we are too preoccupied with the mistakes we just made and fail to see that greater danger is afoot.

God sent his perfect son to die for us. We have already been chosen, but it is our choice that consummates the marriage. We must choose Christ and perpetually deny ourselves. So here I am again, starting from day 1 but with a tuned-up perspective. Never will I be able to walk into a tempting situation purposely and walk out unscathed. That is not how righteousness works. When we accept Christ as our personal savior there are phases of the relationship that must be mastered before true holiness is upon us. Can God trust me to be faithful? Disobedience is too costly. Time is certainly of the essence. Don't procrastinate. It took me seven years to complete a seven-day process, and I have a college degree in finance!

Note well that it is not about our status or educational background, it is about our willingness to endure suffering for his sake. It is our determination to serve God or die that makes us receive true life. Remember that gifts are irrevocable, but gifts are not enough to hear those glorious words, *"well done my good and faithful servant. You may enter into my rest."*

Identity

(After a triumphant year, I had slipped back into my old ways. This is a segment which I had written to myself and I had to pull it back out. One thing I advise to any person is to write! Get a journal. Journaling is like leaving clues to yourself of how to get back home if you ever get lost. This was a major clue that I had left to myself. And it was a prominent player in helping reestablish WHY I had ever given my life to Christ in the first place!)

One of the most important questions a person could ever find the answer to is: ***"Who am I?"*** This is the answer that many people live their entire lives without ever finding. Accurately answering this one question opens the floodgate for any subsequent success, peace, or joy. Our whole lives we search for answers. The problem as I see it is that we are searching for the wrong answers because we have asked the wrong questions.

Your identity is the key component to everything. Without first being molded and told who you are you never have to worry yourself with making any adjustment because you can never get off track when no identity has been given.

"IF YOU DON'T KNOW WHERE YOU'RE GOING, ANY ROAD WILL TAKE YOU THERE." ~ Matt Theriault

Our identities date back to the very beginning of time. We must accept this and understand it well. We must come to the rational resolve that without an "antique referent" as Ravi Zacharias calls it, our lives and our identities are totally relative. Relativism ultimately means that one man is the measure of all things and everyone and everything are judged or classified regarding that man. The question then becomes: Which man shall we choose?

This very personal question of identity is and always will be the quintessential component to finding yourself, learning to love yourself, as well as finding and learning how to love your soul mate. Love is not possible without identity. In my journey, I have found that remaining firm in my identity would prove to be one of my toughest tasks. I still struggle with it at times. Not because I don't know who I am but because I do. When God has a call on your life, it takes you out of the realm of mediocrity and obliterates all levels of comfort. Many of the things I would like to do and say I can no longer partake in.

In fact, what I have found is that when you realize who you are, the people that you felt knew you the best begin to take on a different form.

"WE DO NOT SEE THINGS AS THEY ARE, WE SEE THEM AS WE ARE." ~ Anais Nin

The hardest aspect of change is that people around you who have become comfortable with you in their lives just as you are...have a vested interest in you remaining the same. Change for you will mean change for them. It has been said that 90% of people would rather die than change.

Now that you have read and understood my story, you can imagine how my changing could really impact many people. I made many friends along the way, but they were not convicted to change on the level that I am. As individuals, it is our right to choose our own paths. Freewill is a gift given from God and no one should be able to dictate to us in any facet of our lives. Finding your identity is a personal journey that only you can embark upon. There are no shortcuts and certainly no days off. Figuring out what really motivates you, compels you, stifles growth, or facilitates growth is your responsibility.

One of the most frustrating things that I have found about life is that many of the situations we struggle with were not created by us. The harsh reality though; it's our responsible for breaking those cycles. Identity takes you deep into your own psyche. You probe endlessly into your own heart to understand personal motives and agendas. I have truly been amazed by what I have found out about myself in the last three years of my life.

Every thought, every lesson, every Bible story, every homework assignment is questioned when you probe deep into your soul for answers. There hasn't been a stone left unturned. At one point, I had even arrived at the conclusion that God wasn't real. The bible just didn't make sense. Christians seemed to be the worst people on earth. Nobody was willing to die for their proclaimed faith, and for the life of me I couldn't figure out why every Christian I knew was dirt poor if the God they served had so much opulence. So, I decided that being a Christian just was not a good business move for me.

I studied earnestly for answers to produce a replacement for God. I found nothing that had logical consistency. There were no facts that concretely dispelled what I had learned about God in church. More importantly than anything, there was an uneasiness in me. I never could get any rest. It was like a hint in my soul telling me that God was out there I was just looking in the wrong places.

Finally, I decided to pick up my bible. I had no clue where to begin, so I began in the book of Luke and read about Jesus Christ. What I found, was that the character of Christ, his teachings of the heart of man and his parables hit too close to home to be a coincidence. What is happening in America today is an all-out attempt to totally secularize the entire nation. While other God-less nations are trying to come to God we are trying relentlessly to sever all ties with him. Once my faith was restored, I began to feel convictions about my ways. I began to see that I was completely lost. All that time I had spent trying to deny the existence of God was only causing me to deny my true identity. What we essentially say when we say God doesn't exist is that humanity has no value. We're saying we have no purpose. When you have no identity, it is impossible to fulfill a purpose. What was my purpose?

I entered a covenant with God. *"God if you can still save me, I promise that I will utilize every fiber in me to serve my generation. I will do everything in my power to help a young lady see the tricks and lies of a man who does not have any intention to love them so that they don't end up broken like the women I have encountered in my life."*

There it was. A portion of my purpose revealed to me in that moment. From that point, I knew that if I were to impact the lives of young women and other young men I had to figure out what it meant to be a man. What is man's origin? Why was Man created? When the answers to these questions began to emerge through my prayer and study time, manhood was slowly becoming a part of my identity. For the first time in my life, I began to examine the implications of all my words and actions, how they would affect others' lives and if staying there would be conducive to my process.

Any man that God intends to use must be tested. It is immature and highly unwise for anyone to believe that you will have a testimony that will change lives if you have not been forged by absolute fire. God wants to use people who understand the cost of discipleship to do kingdom empowerment. For a long time, I wanted to believe that salvation wouldn't cost me anything, but that's a misconception propagated by the *"God knows my heart"* indoctrination. Salvation is not free. Sure, it cost us nothing, but it cost Christ everything!

My generation has been programmed to believe that a numerical value is what validates the quality of something, so hearing free induces a feeling of insignificance in our minds. Christ gave his life as an offering for those who believe to be washed in his blood for the remission of their sins.

John 10:30 **"The Father and I are one."**

Just like Christ, we must know without a shadow of a doubt where we come from in order to have and exercise our delegated power. God is infinite; therefore, we draw from an infinite source. There are no limitations or boundaries for those who know who they are.

Mankind is derivative of God, which means that man has god-like abilities but will never exceed the supreme power of the Eternal. If Man ever sobers up, removes the shackles from his mind, and allows God to sanctify him, the world will never forget his name. Our Identity is the substratum to our life. It grants us keys to unlock the very blessings of heaven to bestow upon the earth.

Luke 16:18-19

18 And I tell you, you are Peter [Greek, Petrus—a large piece of rock], and on this rock [Greek, Petra—a huge rock like Gibraltar] I will build my church, and the gates of Hades (the powers of the infernal region) shall not overpower it [or be strong to its detriment or hold out against it].

19 I will give you the keys of the kingdom of heaven, and whatever you bind (declare to be improper and unlawful) on earth must be what is already bound in heaven, and whatever you loose (declare lawful) on earth must be what is already loosed in heaven.

If a man, any man; is willing to humble himself in the presence of God and submit his will into the hands of the Almighty, his true identity will be revealed to him.

Identity is the essential component to becoming a man, woman, or child of God. If you never allow God to take you through your identity phase he will not use you to build his kingdom.

Love has an identity. Without love, there is no life. We were created from love and molded from eternity to serve God through our work. God is unchanging, and his mercies are matchless. The greatest gift to mankind besides the cross of Christ, in my opinion, is the ability to choose. God wrote the end from the beginning, but we have been given the privilege to choose life or death.

I challenge you to choose life. Look deep into your heart and ask yourself, what is my life really about? What purpose will my life serve? Who must I become in order to serve my purpose just as God intended? The kingdom of heaven is certainly upon us. Humanity desperately needs bold souls to stand and fight for Christ. We have shunned his identity, but for the believers, God is still able. Just as he did for me, from a hell-bound sinner to a mighty vessel of truth, God can surely turn it around. This is our invitation to dine with the almighty; R.S.V.P today, tomorrow isn't a guarantee. Don't beat yourself up... but pay close attention to the level of anxiety that haunted me in these last love chronicles.

Closing Doors

Everything that has been given in the previous chronicles all comes to a head here in these final chronicles. You must be willing to close doors. Closing a door is symbolic of keeping unwanted things from entering and safeguarding things that you don't want to leave yet.

Once I came to my senses, all that was left for me to do was close doors. I began to call all the young women of my past and I would explain to them how lost I was and everything that took place between us could hopefully be forgiven. Many turned away, but there were some who were receptive to what I had to say. The most memorable door of all was when Kia called me and asked me **"Why wouldn't you love me the way I loved you?"**

I responded:

"Sweetie, love was never an option for us. I had so many women that were ranked before you, not because of beauty, intellect, or interest, but for the mere fact that they had been waiting in line for years." What we had was passionate and fun, but I couldn't love you because I didn't have any love available. I was running on fumes. My love had been long depleted, and frankly, I didn't know who I was, I just knew what I was. And so did you. That's why you were drawn to me.

Every good woman wants to tame and domesticate the dingo, but that's not how it works. Do you remember the first night I stayed with you? How we talked and loved each other? Wasn't that an awesome night? No expectation, no lies or alibis; just passion. Well, I am a passion professional, but I lack compassion. All that I did was for me. If there was any benefit in it for you, it was fine by me, but it obviously gave you a false sense of hope.

Our time together had nothing to do with me loving you; it had everything to do with the love you found in me. I envied you for that. The way you gave yourself to me freely. The way you trusted me, the way you allowed me to hold you, I knew you were all in. My hope was that your commitment would somehow be transferred or engrafted to my soul. I too wished I could love boldly. You were hope. I needed hope desperately, so I couldn't let you go. I needed you more than you knew!

Please, don't think for a moment that you were not worthy of my love. In fact, it was the exact opposite. I was the one unworthy, and I knew it would only be a matter of time before you realized I was cancer, so I had to do everything in grand fashion. I pray you can forgive me. And thank you for what you were able to give to me. I'll never forget you for it. After a brief silence, she simply said: **"Wow, I had no idea it was that bad for you."** Then there was good-bye. Imagine that, the prey feeling sympathy for the perpetrator. She realized in that moment that I was more lost than she ever had been and that was everything she needed.

This stage of my life was the most liberating. The only thing I had to offer was the truth, so I offered it in abundance. Though it was the most liberating, freedom isn't cheap. I lost much through this process, but what I gained is something that will stay with me for the remainder of my life. I had gained character and began laying the foundation for integrity.

I just closed my last door two days ago. Yes, it seems so cheesy but closing that door has allowed me to finally have a break.

For the first time since kissing Torrie in the second grade, I can say without a hint of hesitation that I am a single man. There are no women that I am obligated to call, text, or spend time with. I have no pregnancy scares stressing me out; I am not worried about anybody calling with any drama. I am a free man, and the feeling is priceless.

But even this freedom was short-lived...

WILL IT EVER STOP?!

Here I sit, it's February 21st, 2017. I am 29 years old. I have not had sex or masturbated in 140 days. I am at peace.

The last year and a half of my life have been absolute hell! Got a minute? I'll explain. It all started at Homecoming 2015. Feeling like the man! We were preparing for our very first tailgate as alums and the energy was booming! I had recently left my old girl, Stoney, and I wasn't over her yet, but I had enough momentum to get me to my next woman without having to reach back out to her. I was ghost!

EVERYTHING was love. The tailgate was going great! We were launching our new sneaker business: Heat Leaked and we were giving away a pair of OVO 10s to help launch the brand!

Diamond

And here comes Diamond...

Hadn't seen or heard from her for at least sixteen months! But when we saw each other, it was magic. I snatched her up, like I do, hugged her tight, and told her to go eat. She did. She loves to eat. Once all the festivities were over and everyone had cleared the yard, I decided to head on back to Rutherfordton.

While on the road, I received a call from a number that I had never seen. Before I could answer they hung up.

Then they called back...

"Hello."

"Hey, George?"

"Yea, who is this?"

"It's me."

"Diamond?!?!"

"Yep."

"Hey!!! Where are you?"

"I'm driving. Heading back home."

"Where is home?"

"Florida."

"Really? How long have you been there? Do you love it?"

"About a year now. Yea, it's ok."

"Well, where are you now?"

"Passing through Charlotte..."

"Yo! Me too! I'm on 85 South."

"I just passed the Tyvola Rd exit."

"I'm only a few minutes away. I'm coming to see you"

We met at the McDonald's. When she got out of the car, we just hugged...

We sat in my car and talked for hours! I could tell she didn't want to leave. I didn't want her to go either. So, I suggested we get a hotel room for the night and head out in the morning. She was down. So that's what we did. Once we got there, I already knew what was on my mind. But I wanted to slow play it to see where she was.

We ended up falling asleep without any action, but that next morning I was acting. As soon as I woke up, from hardly sleeping because I wanted to have sex the whole night, I started eating it. She still didn't want to really give it up! I am persistent though. To be honest, and frank, I would never rape a young woman, but I have been in some situations that give me a clear insight into how it could go down. And I'm not speaking of brutally beating a woman, ripping her clothes off and taking it, I'm speaking of a passive-aggressive approach in which we practically beg until they let us put the head in.

Once it's in, it pretty much is a done deal from there. After our very brief episode, we packed up and left out. Our next stop was CVS to pick up a plan B. Which is funny because the whole night, I talked to her about how much I wanted a child and how ready I was. As soon as I thought of the commitment involved with a child, I was right back to my old self. I hadn't changed.

That day, she said to me, *"George, if you are involved with any other women, let's just go slow. I'm back, and there is no need to rush."* Without hesitation, I said **"NO! I ain't got nobody!"**

LIES!!!! I kissed and hugged her. She got into her car after I made sure she took the plan B pill. I had to play like it wasn't a big deal, but it was. Then we both headed out.

I went straight to Bella's house. Remember Bella? Yea... she's still bae at this point too. Had sex with her that morning before heading to church. Not an hour later, I was texting Diamond about how excited I was to see her and how much I had enjoyed spending time with her the night before. From that point, Diamond came up to see me nearly every weekend. My family was happy to see her back around. She fit in. She even spent Thanksgiving with us. Keep in mind, she and I are right at one month of being reunited. Already "in love" already talking kids and a family. By Christmas, I was having FaceTime sex with another woman and had had sex with Stoney a few nights as well.

STONEY

You don't know about Stoney. She is the woman that I was in love with right before the month leading up to Homecoming. She and I had been together for about a year or so, after being friends for about eight to ten months before. She was EVERYTHING. Gorgeous skin, amazing hair, brilliant, great conversationalist. You name it, she had it! She was a tad naïve, but it was cool because it made her extremely helpful.

The real deal is that my mama liked her from the jump. I hadn't decided because her butt wasn't fat enough for me. She came into my life and things took off! I got a new job. Income tripled. She helped draw out the outline for these chronicles and she also was an integral piece in my Startup. She was so impactful in fact, that everyone in my life noticed the changes that were taking place.

Stoney was Walmart. She had everything I needed. I was all in. I wanted to marry her! Dang near immediately. But she was only 23 when we met, and it was too overwhelming. For some reason, when I was with Stoney I had this extremely powerful conviction on me to not have sex with her. I was hooked and couldn't stop though. She was the best I had ever had, in every aspect. I was the same for her or at least I wanted to believe that.

This was one of those scary connections like she had hijacked my soul or something. I was so afraid because she was able to speak things about my life that she couldn't have known. Which I later found was witchcraft! She doesn't believe in the Bible. At the time I couldn't put my finger on it...Like that night she and I were in the hotel, she didn't even know about Diamond, but she spoke of it as if I had told her every detail. So, I just concluded that she was a demon or witch; something! I couldn't explain it, but I knew it was uncanny. At the time, dismissing it was more convenient than trying to figure it out. Now that you know Stoney, let me get back to Diamond. I kid you not, Diamond and I were reunited at Halloween, in love by Thanksgiving, seriously talking marriage by Christmas but weren't even on speaking terms by Valentine's Day. As a matter of fact, February 1st was the last time we sat and talked face up. But Y'all know me… I'm moving on.

BROKEN BUT STILL PRETENDING

Honestly, I'm in hell at this point. Don't know if I am coming or going! I can't seem to figure anything out. Frustrated. Feeling hopeless. Just not knowing where I'm supposed to be in life. Or if life is even the right thing for me anymore. I was stuck! Desperate for ANYTHING that made even a little sense. Desperate for someone to understand me! Surely there had to be a woman somewhere who could feel me!

Just when I had nearly lost hope, I got this Facebook notification from a fine, thick, chocolate lady named Mac! As soon as I saw the notification I inboxed her: *"movie date?"* She said "No." Just as I suspected she would, but I had planted the seed. I knew she was interested, she liked the post. I only needed to be persistent. From there it began. I continued to hit her up. She continued to reject every advance that I made. Then one day, there was a breakthrough! It was a Saturday. She was at the salon getting her hair done, I had driven to Charlotte with the sole purpose of getting her to let me come see her, and if she said no, I already had a day set with a young lady in Greensboro.

It was a win-win situation. Unfortunately, these are the only types of situations that men in our generation look for. "Win-Win" that is. We can't stand the thought of putting our best foot forward and being rejected! I was at a point where I wanted to avoid hard work, pain, and confrontation. I wanted a connection so grand that I forgot about all my struggles. And wouldn't you know it? After some digging, I found that Mac wanted the same thing.

One night, around 10 pm, she got hungry. I drove up to take her to eat. That night we nearly had sex. She said, **"No, I don't want this relationship to go like all of the ones in my past."** This should have triggered something in my mind. It didn't!

Two nights later, I was right back, and you better believe I hit them chocolate buns! A month later, I transferred my job and moved in with her. One month!!! All because we "connected." In my previous two relationships, I was certain that both of those women were crazy! Naw bruh, I was about to experience a level of crazy that I thought only existed in movies. After only two months of shacking, I had been kicked out three times, left on my own twice and slept on the couch once. The day that broke the bough came one night after she had gone through my phone and saw that I had told a young lady that she was

"beautiful and that her life was going to be good because she was awesome".

In my mind, this was generic, friendship encouragement stuff. In her mind, it was the ultimate deception. The entire day she and I went back and forth. I couldn't work. So, I left. When I got home, of course she was cool, calm, and collected. At this point though, I'm hot! I strike up the argument. It escalated quickly! She threatened to call her daddy to have him come "beat my ass"

I responded, *"you better call your brother, your daddy doesn't have a chance, he's too old"*

Just so you know, prior to this moment I had never cussed around her. This was the first time she had seen me being belligerently aggressive. Naturally, it alarmed her. Not to mention I propped my finger on her forehead just to let her know that she had no authority or power. Then she turned and went to the drawer by the bed, reached in, grabbed her gun, cocked and told me to *"Get the Fuck out"*!

I had never had a gun pulled on me. I had only seen it in the movies, but my reaction was a lot different than I imagined it would've been. It infuriated me. I urged her to kill me!!! The fact that she now had the power in that moment irked me!!! So much so that the preservation of life had totally escaped me.

Besides, this would have cured my embarrassment of moving back in with my pops and mama. The embarrassment of my family witnessing as another relationship dwindled to nothing, I had reached a point in my life where they would all know, it is not the women. It's George.

"George is the one with the issues."

Her killing me, or at least shooting me felt like my only way out! In the moment, shame was tougher to handle than death. The thought of lasting, insurmountable shame provokes thoughts of suicide. Don't believe me? Well, you should. It's the truth. I know because I had to wrestle with it... One evening I was in the kitchen preparing a banana pudding for Mac. I knew she had a gun in the kitchen drawer in addition to the one she pulled on me. The thought just continued to cross my mind *"take it out and do it. It won't last long. It won't even hurt. Just do it."*

What's sad is, I wanted to! I really wanted to! But just like that day when she pulled the gun, I thought of my pops and how he'd given his life so that my sister and I could live better. In both instances, I knew he wouldn't be able to wrap his mind around how this could have happened. I may as well have taken the gun and shot him. Had it not been for my Pops, I probably would've done it.

I was miserable. There was this seemingly perfect woman that my entire family, both sides, liked a lot. I was earning nearly $80,000. I was 28. I was young, good-looking, healthy, smart, funny, amiable, caring, sharing, giving, loving. You name it. I had it! BUT I HAD NO PEACE. I had let go of obedience. I had forsaken the word of God. He wasn't working fast enough and at times didn't even seem to care! I needed a breakthrough, and if He wasn't going to send it, I was going to create it.

As I stood there, gun in her hand, I thought about my pops. I turned and walked out. What I had not realized was the fact that I had become dependent on her. I was in a new city, had a new job location, and nowhere to stay. So, I went back. I continued to justify. I blamed myself. It was my fault she had pulled the gun out. She was scared. She had never seen me act that way before, she had to protect herself.

All these things in my mind kept me tied to this woman. Then it hit me; I was in a verbally abusive relationship. Of all people, me, George Hines Jr. was being verbally abused. But it was true. Her inherent distrust in men because of the deeply seeded disappointments she'd experienced from her father her entire life caused her to believe the only way she could keep a man was to beat him down to a place where only her love could comfort him. She was good. She had attained a level of mastery. And for me, I had almost been consumed by it.

On her end what she had encountered, was a young man who had mastered the art of connection. I know how to connect to a woman on any level. I understand how to hack into their mentality to get in their space. Once in their space, depending on the amount of desperation I was experiencing at the moment, I could take it to any level.

With her, I had taken it so far that I nearly had to pay with my life. This is the destruction of disobedience. And it nearly stole my life.

FULL CIRCLE

Ironically, the young lady who helped me structure these Chronicles is the very point at which new revelation began. After finally swallowing my pride and moving back home with my parents, I began to pray and look back over my life...What happened to me?!!! I was happy. Things were good! How did I get so far off track again? I began digging back through my journals, Instagram posts, and Facebook posts. By doing this, maybe I could hone in on the context that created all the greatness in my life. Who was there, what purpose they served, and how impactful they were?

Stoney was there right around that point. That is where I began. What I found around the time I was with Stoney was that my prayer and study time was on point. My confidence was flourishing. I had a purpose. I had passion. I had an identity. But once I stepped away from those things, I lost my way again.

In life, we'll get lost. That's life. Realizing you are lost is the challenge. If you can come to that realization, you can begin to retrace your steps. Where you lost it is where you will find it. From there is where you'll rebuild and rediscover who you are and why you are here.

Whenever we are finished experimenting. God is ready to give us a life.

ADVICE TO MY 20-YEAR-OLD SELF

At the age of 20, I knew what my life was going to be. Now, at 29 I realize I was completely wrong about every detail! When I look back on my life it brings me to tears... Not because I'm particularly sad for myself, but because I'm sad for all the young 20 somethings coming up now with the same misplaced sense of self. We are a generation of young people who all long to be known for something great. I'm no exception.

My advice to 20-year-old George:

Fail quicker. Don't settle for a decent life. Go for it all or leave it all alone. But you must understand that going for it all requires working through major uncertainties. The moment your desire for high income exceeds your desire to be processed you've already lost.

The process always proceeds greatness. 20 G leave these girls alone!!!! You're not going to get it right because you're not ready. Focus on yourself. Focus on your business. Become a man who can stand on his own feet. Don't allow the doubts and limitations in others minds to hinder your growth.

You'll come to find that your friends don't really know how to be friends. They love you. And they'll do anything for you, but that won't get you to the next level. Stop talking about doing something great and commit to doing something now! Don't allow the anxieties created by hyper-ambition and social media to make you feel incompetent. Create our own lane. You can't win their race; no matter how fast you are. You'll only lose yourself.

Stay in the moment. Your past will rule your present and cancel your future. I know... I'm a product of it. Take control of your life by taking control of your environment. Nostalgia is the enemy. Faith makes the moment BIG! Big moments are necessary if you truly desire a big life. Don't ever let your days become so routine that you don't have to think. There must be a healthy amount of surprise in your life.

Do something each day that makes you nervous. Something that will make people question your sanity. Sing louder. Dance harder. Fight (for truth that is). Whatever path you choose, go 100%. Giving less than 100% of yourself is nothing more than an attempt to pretend that you're something you're not!

NEVER WORK A JOB! You were not made for jobs.

Success requires failures.

When you strive for the impossible, you'll find that you're greater than you could ever imagine. Figure out how to let go. When your hands are full of old hurt you can't receive new joy. Be a man. Say what you truly feel. Holding back is never going to work for you anyway.

Call the girl with the big hair. Yes, the one in the red shirt and tell her how much you really love her... Tell her that she has been the fire behind it all. But you have got to let that go little bruh. She's not coming back. Don't miss another good one because you can't let go. Yes. She's got it going on, but you're the man too.

Show your sister more love. She's going to need it. You don't have to worry about your cousin Whit, she's going to find a great man who's going to give her everything she's ever needed. You're going to be surprised at who it is too. *(hahaha)* Pops is gone be pops. Keep encouraging ma, she's greater than she knows. And on the evening of December 9, 2016, tell her to stay and help granny fix the Christmas tree, then hug her tightly.

Oh, don't cross the line with Riley. She won't be able to let what's going to happen between you go. Don't make Jojo have the abortion. You're still regretting that one. And when you play against Delaware State, go down. Don't take that hit! Most importantly 20 G, figure out who God is bruh and how big the cross of Jesus Christ really is. I got to go man. But take heed to my words. You'll be glad you listened. Time flies 20 G. Can't wait to see you grow.

Sincerely, 29 G.

NO LONGER PRETENDING

It's November 2017. In two minutes it'll be Riley's birthday, (go figure). But she wasn't the reason for this moment. This moment came at the hands of an old friend of mine who just posted pictures of Porsha's baby shower. Yes, Porsha is pregnant with a child and about to get married. And instead of the information being heartbreaking, it was liberating.

A few months back when I was writing to my 20-year-old self about her, none of this was going on. Or at least I wasn't aware of it. Anyway, I was looking at the only woman I have ever wanted to love in the eyes as she happily posed for one of the biggest photos of her life. I even messaged her to congratulate her a short while back. She seems happy. But I think she settled. Of course, I have a very biased opinion. But what do I know? I'm a soon to be 30-year-old man who lives at home with his parents, with no money. Well, no I lied. I have $8.59. Earlier I had a whopping $50!!!!

I was going to give it to my cousin who loaned me the $7000 to help me jumpstart my sneaker company that I still believe is going to be groundbreaking, it just hasn't gained traction yet. There was a lady at the gas station who was literally counting pennies to get gas for her car.

Being in the very same predicament just a week or so ago, I felt her pain. So, I gave her $10. What the heck? A fifty-dollar payment on a $7000 debt is enough to piss a person off anyway. And I'm going to get back to Porsha and love, but I want to paint this picture for all my readers. Social Media has done our generation a major disservice in presenting the entrepreneurial lifestyle as glamorous and fun.

It's been *everything* but thus far! I have $22,000 dollars in credit card debt on a card that only has a $20,000 limit. I haven't made a car payment in 3 months and the only reason they haven't repoed it is because I used to work at the Credit Union that gave me the loan. That and the loan officer likes me.

My car insurance is about to lapse. Student loans are in default. Cell phones are only on because my pops and sister wanted to keep their phones on and I just happen to be on the same plan with them. Oh, and I put my two weeks' notice in at my job 3 weeks ago. Not because I don't need the money, but because I just don't care about anything but my fingers stroking these keys and people being set free. I know what you're thinking... "you're a lazy bum! And you're an idiot! *(Long pause for emphasis)* I see why Porsha or any other woman ain't checking for you!" And you're probably right.

But deep down inside of me, there is this unwavering assurance that everything is going to be incredibly amazing. I'm not happy with how everything in my life has turned out up until this point, but I'm optimistic about where it's going. My faith in God has not wavered. Hearing the news about Porsha made me think back to last summer when I saw her for the first time in nearly 4 years. She teared up. That's a great feeling when the woman you would give it all up for is happy to see you. We hung out for days. I savored every moment. Not once did I make any sexual advances, nor did I think about it.

That taught me an invaluable lesson: **when a man is ready to love a woman, I mean really ready to love her, he won't risk losing her for self-gain.** Her honor meant more to me than my pleasure did.

That hasn't been the case with other women in the last years. Everything I have written to you here has been a rollercoaster ride I know, but you're only reading. Imagine living it... Imagine having Billion-dollar potential that everyone sees, but you don't know how to tap into it. Imagine having women give their best efforts to make you see that loving them would be worthwhile and only being able to think about the one woman who doesn't seem to care at all. If you don't take anything from my story, be sure to write this down: **"You choose! Don't allow life to choose for you."** Indecision is the decision that proves you're not ready to be great.

Because I was afraid of being vulnerable. Because I wouldn't honor the process. Because I wanted to present a secure man to the world when I was merely a broken-hearted boy who suppressed my frustrations, I kept missing my turn.

I'm not saying that Porsha and I were supposed to be together. What I am saying is that it wasn't her job to choose me. It was my job to choose her. My lack of focus, my inconsistencies, and my pride all got in the way of what my heart was trying desperately to reveal to me. Be brave enough to go after what matters to you in life. No matter how crazy it makes you look. In the end, you'll be better for it. I have never in my life regretted the chances that I have taken, only the chances I was too afraid to take.

I hope every young man who can read gets his hands on this book. I hope he can feel my anguish and frustrations as he flips through the pages. I hope that all the young women realize that you will be the ruins of a man who has no understanding of manhood if you do not stay clear. All the sex. All the lies. The pregnancy scares. The STD scares. The abortions. All the hurt women. All the deceit. It didn't amount to anything. But it cost me some of the most prime years of my life. And sure, people will say, "If you hadn't gone through it, you wouldn't be who you are!" Well of course not! That's the point!

We don't have to be the recovering addict, so we'll have a cool story to tell. If I could be on the other end of this information, I'd switch places in a second. Not because I hate my journey, but because I hate the fact that I passed on wisdom to trade years of my life for the same knowledge; we call it experience. Other people's lives are assets to us if we take the time to pull the truth from it. We don't have to make the same mistakes all the men or women in our families made. God has blessed me with an amazing gift of storytelling. For years, I abused it. All I wanted was some new coochie, so everybody would think I was the man.

Now, I only want manhood.

I only want what God has for me. Don't spend all your money and youth chasing a life that was never meant for you. One of two things will happen:

1. The lifestyle will become the prison that ultimately puts you to death

2. You'll lose interest in it once you get it, because it will not fill the void.

And make no mistakes about it, it's your fight. No one is coming to save you. If you're going to have a great life, it's up to you. If you are ever going to escape the lethal grasp of adolescence and grab hold to manhood, you must fight daily and if necessary, be willing to die. Submit your will to God young brother. Be very cautious young sister. It only takes one heartbreak, one act of ignorance to consume your years.

Finishing this book allows me to end a phase of my life that has been drawn out entirely too long. One big vicious cycle leading right back to more misery and confusion; hell. Lastly, always keep an open mind. You never know what God is going to use to bring abundance into your life. Look at me, all those years of being mean to my sister and having to write those word reports turned me into an author.

God truly has a sense of humor and knows how to heal the hearts of his children. What does it mean to be Healed? Heal – Cause a wound, injury, or person to become sound or healthy again. *(Google search for Heal definition)* To heal we must be able to accept what was, understand what is, and prepare ourselves for what's to come.

Most people get stuck like I did and live the same year over and over and over. Not realizing that's what they're doing because they have become numb to the pain and disillusioned by their meager successes. Life is no cake walk. It will devour you and spit you back out. Healing requires maturity. To heal you must have stable people around you who can be truthful with you. More importantly, you must be able to receive correction.

If any amount of pride ever creeps in, you can forget about being healed properly.

"Prideful healing" better known as *unforgiveness* will never allow you to get the full range of motion you once had. It's kind of like breaking a bone and never having it set in its proper place for it to heal correctly, so that limb never really functions the same again. When we won't be healed we put others at risk. Hurt people are highly infectious. They go around spreading their hurt to any and every environment that refuses to suffocate them.

People who refuse to be healed need attention. They need commotion around constantly. If the noise on the outside ever silences, then they will have to deal with all the noise on the inside. So, they run, never stopping to realize that no matter where they go, they will be there. Healing requires quiet time. It requires some isolation and separation. Once a person is healed though, they are going to love themselves so much more for not quitting. That's when they can begin to live again.

Like my man Drake says, "more life".

Thank you for hearing my story.

Next stop, Manhood.

Epilogue

Hardships are defined as *severe suffering or privation* by dictionary.com. I believe hardships are so much more. We must be willing to dig deeper. For 10 years I practically hated myself for not being able to rid my mind of the memories and my heart of the emotions I had for a particular young woman. Throughout those 10 years I saw myself as pitiful, incompetent, and foolish. Now that I have taken a step back, regained my confidence, and rediscovered my value, I see very differently.

I haven't been weak all those years. I had been loyal. Which for me, is shocking! During my times of debauchery, "loyal" is a description that I would grudgingly assign to my character. What I have discovered about seeing correctly is that accurate vision requires forgiveness.

Being unforgiving infected me on many levels. My inability to concede the fact that I too, can be hurt and disappointed propelled me in a storm of selfishness that consumed everyone in my path. There are so many young women who get a bad taste in their mouths when they hear my name.

I hope that they can learn from my denial. The only way out is to own it and walk through it. Everything that goes wrong in our lives will not be our fault, but it is our sole responsibility to fix it.

So often, the negative perception we have of our past smothers any ensuing good that could potentially come from the same place. Understanding the value of holistic thinking gave me the objectivity that was necessary to stop blaming and begin healing.

There is nothing in this world that can stop us. Only thought has the power to catapult us forward or consign us to a life of mediocrity.

As we train our minds to think right, we unconsciously induce wellness in our lives.

"Forgive to Live"

ACKNOWLEDGMENTS

There are some many people that I want to thank for helping me become the man that I am today. Though I won't mention every single person here, you know exactly who you are, and I want to sincerely thank you!

First, I want to thank pops. From the time I was a boy, I have memories of you reading to me and instilling an unwavering sense of confidence in me. You gave me the truth and continually fostered that truth so that I would never deny it or ignore it. This for me was the most valuable component. Making you proud has been my chief aim forever! Even as a grown man, I'm still "looking up in the stands" to make sure you see me when I do something good. You set the bar high. That's why I can't settle. So. If my choices don't make sense, it's because you made me believe I could do anything; be anything. And I do believe.

Next, Ma. More than anything in the universe you cared about our souls finding rest in the Lord. No, it's not as riveting (at first thought) as an MLB ballplayer but finding Christ has been the best thing that has ever happened. And you get that credit. Those nights you woke us up as you marched up and down the halls praying, covering our home will never be forgotten. For forcing me to read all those pages all those days. I don't know how you were so good at being a mama, but I thank you!

Pastor Twitty! My goodness. I can't say enough about the man you are. Your integrity and rawness have cultivated my life in ways that no other person on the planet could have. People often ask me, *"George, why don't you get away from*

Rutherford County?" They just didn't know there was a prophet in the land. Leaving your covenant and spiritual fatherhood would've been suicide. I can't thank you enough for stretching me. You demanded greatness. You demanded professionalism. You gave us no room for excuses and you back up everything with the Word of God. I'm blessed to be your spiritual son. Without you, I'd be a rich fool with a ton of education but no wisdom. You taught me to appreciate the journey and slow down. Thank you for seeing the best in me when I couldn't find it in myself.

To my sister, thank you for being you. You know, what's funny? Had I been more loving to you from an early age, I doubt this book would've ever made it to the world. Thank you for not hating me. As I grow more in understanding, my love for you grows as well. Thank you for making me an uncle. It's Heavenly!

To my uncles: Tommy, Ed, Barry, Ken, Ty, Pinchy, Hank, Terry, Ronnie. From aspiring to be 6'4 like uncle Crawf, to the gold sweat suit, all the way down to Rutherford little league.

Each of you have played an integral part in my manhood. Thank you all for being real men.

To Rah, big bruh, you were more insightful about my future than I was. I'll never forget that night you made me stay in the front room as y'all slipped out to the back room. That night is the reason why I've still never touched drugs or alcohol to this day.

To all my cousins. "Luh y'all"!

Keith, some people think Strong Boys, Fragile Men could be a best seller! I might finally be able to pay you back some of the million dollars I owe you from my food tab.

Felicia, you're Wonder Woman.

Whitney, from the time we were little you've been down for whatever. I can't even begin to imagine how my life would have been without you.

To my little itty-bitty baby cousin Janiya, you are the blessing that no one could've predicted. You're growing into an amazing young woman. Read lots of books!!! Ask lots of questions!!!

To Strap, Willie, CJ Beatty, Billy Enright, TJ Edison Hearns, Randy, BJ, Billionaire P, and X-man. Thank you for being my brothers.

Special thanks to Mrs. A&T for writing my forward and afterword (which I didn't use. Sorry). Moreover, thank you for your time, open heart and listening ear. You're sitting in the important people section at my wedding.

To Mrs. Fuller-Miller you saved my life a long time ago. Your love, compassion, and devotion as a teacher got me through. I doubt you've had any greater impact on a third grader's life.

To Mrs. Pittman, thank you for entering me in that writing contest my senior year. I felt lame and dorky, but it showed me way back then that writing was a skill that could lead to some great opportunities.

Coach Shumate, thank you for giving me a chance to prove myself. That's all any man could ever ask for; a chance.

Finally, and most importantly. I want to thank God for saving my soul! In you, I live, move, and have my being.

Notes

Who is George Hines Jr.
- John 8:32 ERV
- "Truth is the most valuable thing in the world..."
  G.K Chesterson
- "Truth is incontrovertible..."
  Winston Churchill

Wake Up Call
- Romans 8:28 The Voice translation

Chronicles of Love
   Zora
- "Bool People Buss" From the hit HBO series Insecure writer Issa Rae utilizes the phrases.

My 7-year Struggle
- "Sometimes it takes 10 years to get that one year that will change your life."   ~
  Unknown
- Luke 11:24-26 Amplified

Finding Your Rib
- "I know you wanna leave me..." lyrics; Temptations 'Ain't to Proud to Beg' 1966
- "Love T.K.O." Teddy Pendergrass
- "At Last! This one is bone of my bone..."
  Genesis 2:23 The Voice
- "It is not good that man is alone..."
  Genesis 2:18 The Voice
- Matthew 19:4-5 NLT

What is Love?
- Ephesians 5:25-28 The Message Translation
- "Lust is your desire for something or someone that is not intended for you"
- Genesis 3:6,23-24 ERV
- 1 John 2:16 NLT
- John 3:16 NLT

Creative Imagination
- "The desire for sex expression" Sex Transmutation, Think and Grow Rich
- 2 Corinthians 5:17 New King James Version
- Ephesians 2:2 WEB
- Isaiah 14: 11-17 ERV
- Ezekiel 28:12-19 ERV
- Romans 12:2 ERV

My Fragmented Soul

"there is nothing enlightened about shrinking…"
   Marianne Williamson, Our Deepest Fear
The Loneliest Journey
- Commitment definition. Merriam and Webster's Dictionary
- "Be fruitful and multiply" Genesis 1:28 NLT
- Ephesians 5:25-26 The Voice
The Resurgence of Impatience
- "Well done my good and faithful servant, you shall enter into my rest." Matthew 25:23, Hebrews 4:1
Identity
- "If you don't know where you're going, any road will take you there." Matt Theriault, 'The Epic Real Estate Investing Show'
- "We don't see things as they are, we see them as we are." Anais Nin
- Luke 16:18-19 Amplified
- John 10:30 God's Word Translation

Made in the USA
Columbia, SC
29 August 2018